"Presence: A Guide to Transforming Your M̶ lating selection of the "tips" that Ann Weiser Cor̶n̶e̶l̶l̶,̶ t̶h̶e̶ j̶o̶.̶.̶.̶.̶.̶.̶.̶.̶.̶.̶ .̶ g in the English-speaking world today, has been sending weekly for years to her many online followers. Each tip responds to a real question from a particular individual, yet all of them touch on universal themes, ranging from depression and avoidance to relationship challenges, anger, and feelings of shame and self-criticism. The key to resolving all of these challenges lies in our ability to be truly, lovingly present to ourselves — "Self-in-Presence" Ann calls it—and this book shows us how to culti-vate this invaluable inner skill. Presence is a user-friendly book, beautifully de-signed and illustrated, and written with Ann's characteristic clarity, directness, and warmth. It is a true feast for the soul, full of wise and practical recipes for living a fuller and happier life."

— DAVID I. ROME, author of *Your Body Knows the Answer: Using Your Felt Sense to Solve Problems, Effect Change, and Liberate Creativity*

"Emotional health lies not with arguing against, overcoming or "rising above" our emotions, but with understanding what they are trying to tell us, and using their enormous power constructively. In this lovely, warm, and elegantly written book, Ann Weiser Cornell shows people how they can "be with" even the most difficult and challenging emotional states and life situations and come out the other side richer, wiser, stronger, and more able to go forward in their lives. Reading this book is like having Ann's warm, reassuring voice right next to you showing you the way to reach the nuggets of wisdom and transformation within. It should be every Focuser's Focusing companion!"

— HELENE G. BRENNER, PH.D., Psychologist & Author of *I Know I'm in There Somewhere: A Woman's Guide to Finding Her Inner Voice and Living a Life of Authenticity*

"Accessible yet deep, Presence is an important book about taking care of our emotions and understanding how they can be transformed. In her genuine and warm-hearted style, Ann Weiser Cornell answers practical questions from real people about their struggles with challenging emotions. Readers facing all kinds of difficulties – from compulsive eating and addictions to making difficult decisions – will be able to use Ann's wisdom to learn how to embrace and transform their emotions without blocking or suppressing them."

— ANNIE MAHON, author of the blog *rawmindfulness.com* and the book, *Things I Did When I Was Hangry: Navigating a Peaceful Relationship with Food*

PRESENCE:

A GUIDE TO TRANSFORMING YOUR MOST CHALLENGING EMOTIONS

Ann Weiser Cornell

 CALLUNA PRESS

PUBLISHER'S NOTE:

This publication is designed to provide accurate and authoritative information in regard to the subject matter covered. It is sold with the understanding that the publisher is not engaged in rendering psychological, financial, legal, or other professional services. If expert assistance or counseling is needed, the services of a competent professional should be sought.

Copyright © 2015 Ann Weiser Cornell

Calluna Press
2560 Ninth Street, Ste 315-A
Berkeley, CA 94710
510.225.0690

Design and layout: Maggie Hurley
Text Formatting: Shannon Crossman
Content Editor: Brittany Dean

ISBN 978-0-9721058-4-2

TABLE OF CONTENTS

APPRECIATIONS

Many people helped make this book a reality. At the top of the list is my dear friend and collaborator of more than 20 years, Barbara McGavin.

BARBARA MCGAVIN

Barbara and I met in 1991, both Focusing teachers, and from that very first meeting there was a creative spark as we discovered that we had been thinking along the same lines about what people really need to get deep emotional transformation. We co-developed an approach to Focusing called Inner Relationship Focusing. A few years later, when we both faced some of the biggest challenges of our lives, our friendship and working partnership enabled us to not just get through those challenges, but to actually create a transformational method for finding emotional healing and fresh life possibilities in life's most difficult problems. The process we created, which we now call Untangling (also known as Treasure Maps to the Soul), can be found throughout this book. For example, the concept of Self-in-Presence is from the Untangling work.

I say that "we" created the Untangling process — and that is true but many of the ideas came first from Barbara. There is no way that this book would have existed without Barbara. Our ongoing collaboration has illuminated my life in countless ways.

Next I need to thank all the people whose questions to me made this book possible. Your courageous sharing of your struggles, with the specific detail that makes the questions so easy to relate to, were absolutely essential, and I'm humbly grateful. I had conversations with other Focusing teachers, dear friends and colleagues, who helped me clarify what I wrote in these Tips. Most notably: Lucinda Hayden, a gifted collaborator and fabulous teacher whose ability to hold a big vision supports this work on every level; Helene Brenner, a remarkable healer and teacher with a leading-edge ability to understand the depths of process; Stefan Ebert, whose sensitivity and intelligence go to the heart of what matters.

I stand in deep awe and gratitude to my amazing team here at Focusing Resources — Shannon Crossman, Brittany Dean, Maggie Hurley — I list them in alphabetical order because there is no way to classify their priceless contributions. Maggie gets a special mention for designing the book so beautifully and finding most of the illustrations. Shannon flowed the text into the book which was a monumental task, and held the whole project with her unmatched gifts for moving things forward. Brittany is the one who sifted through over 400 tips to select the 43 we used in this book and also contributed her fine-tuned sense for just the right note in both design and editing.

And we're all grateful to L. Herrada-Rios whose support in the office made the work on this book possible, including answering the phone so the rest of us could keep on task.

My daughter Mika also contributed with great conversations and emotional support, and, as always, first and last, my beloved life partner Joe McBride.

Ann Weiser Cornell

This book was created for people who need help and support to find a better relationship with their own challenging emotions. When emotions knock us over, we can't think clearly or act wisely, and we suffer.

But the solution is not to suppress our emotions, because then we lose what makes us human <u>and</u> we lose some of the vital information to help us make wise choices. Also, emotions that are suppressed remain unchanged...but so do emotions that are allowed to run wild and take us over.

People struggle with shame, anxiety, rage, frustration... To feel, to try not to feel, to feel less, to hide what we feel from others...and if the struggle has gone on for years, people also struggle with hopelessness that it could ever be another way.

Well, it can. With Inner Relationship Focusing (also called Focusing) there is definitely another way.

This book is a selection of the questions asked me by real people struggling with emotion-related issues over the last five years, and my answers. We've grouped them into sections: Intense Feelings, Decisions and Frustration, The Trouble with Feeling Happy, Emotion Wars, Avoiding Feelings, Anxiety and Anger, Unfulfilled Desire and Relationships, Shame and Self-Criticism, Overwhelm and Tears — Identifying with Parts, Trauma, and, finally, Good Feelings.

These questions and answers originally appeared in a Weekly Tips email newsletter. In that newsletter, I could assume that my readers shared some background information and awareness of concepts like 'Focusing,' 'Self-in-Presence,' 'parts' and the like. I want to take a bit of time to explain those concepts here so that you, the reader, can get the most out of this book.

Focusing is simple: You invite the bodily feel of any situation that troubles you and offer it non-judging awareness, and it then opens up into insight and positive life change. But Focusing may not seem simple because it is truly revolutionary—it turns our usual cultural assumptions on their heads.

For example, we usually think:

- We have to fix ourselves or get someone to fix us — but actually, positive change is inherent in us if we learn how to give ourselves a certain kind of attention and get out of our own way.

- We have to get over or get past our emotional states — especially the 'ugly' ones like fear or shame — but actually, even the very 'worst' feelings contain gifts of positive energy, if we turn toward them with compassion and curiosity.

- Our bodies are purely physical and that intelligence is in the brain and the mind — but actually, the body process as felt from the inside is much vaster and wiser than the intellect alone.

Focusing was developed by Eugene Gendlin out of research into successful psychotherapy yet its uses have gone far beyond therapy, really into every area of life. Basically Focusing is something you can do — in any moment of your life — to shift your relationship to whatever is going on, and also something you can do in quiet, meditation-like sessions to explore and bring change to your challenging life issues. If you'd like to know more about how to do Focusing, we have suggestions at the end of this book.

Knowing how to do Focusing is not required for you to make use of this book, but it may help to know that in Focusing you invite the body feel of what you are going through, something we call a 'felt sense.' You then bring acceptance and curiosity to this felt sense, and you experience steps of insight and relief.

Inner Relationship Focusing is a version of Focusing developed by Barbara McGavin and myself in order to make Focusing even more effective for emotion-based life issues. Inner Relationship Focusing includes the whole Focusing process as Gendlin set it out, and adds methods and concepts for working with parts and enhancing wholeness.

Parts are temporary aspects of the self that emerge when our full self is not available to handle emotional states or solve life problems. By their very nature, parts are at odds with each other, and so we experience painful inner conflict. We may find ourselves saying, for example, "Part of me wants to give up on this relationship because it's too painful, but another part of me is hanging on and won't let go."

Protector parts (sometimes called 'controlling' parts) are parts that are worried about you and often express that worry through criticism and blame. **Defender parts** are parts that are rebellious or crushed, and may be impulsive and self-indulgent. **The Small One** is a type of part that holds a frozenness around an old trauma and is either hidden away or painfully retriggered by current events.

Self-in-Presence (also called Presence) is the most important concept in this book. In the first few Tips in the book I describe how to cultivate Self-in-Presence. Almost every other Tip adds to an understanding of how to bring Self-in-Presence to a current issue.

Self-in-Presence is the ability to turn toward our challenging emotions rather than being caught up in them. You will hear me talk about "giving company" to your feelings or "being with" your emotional states. It may help to re-read page 15 when you forget what this means or you aren't sure how to do it. For example, one way to give company to your emotional state is to let a gentle hand move to the place in your body where you feel it. You can say, "I am with you," or "I am here." This isn't always easy...and many of the questions in the pages that follow are from people who found Self-in-Presence challenging. I hope I helped them!

And most of all I hope this book helps you, dear reader. Do let me know. I'm still answering questions—with pleasure!

Ann Weiser Cornell
Berkeley, California, USA

DO YOU FEEL LIKE YOU ARE ADDICTED TO SADNESS, LONGING AND SELF-PITY?

"I am addicted to sadness, longing, self-pity, wishing, dreaming, etc..."

Recently I identified myself as being addicted to the emotion of sadness, and all of the concomitant feelings/behaviors like longing, self-pity, wishing, dreaming, etc. Coming from an alcoholic home, I retreated often, drew inward to a sad place that was at least safe. My life choices all seem to have taken me to one sad situation after another. And other very unhappy life circumstances like the death of my young child many years ago have kept me stuck in this sad place.

Now I find myself working toward divorce from my second husband, a very functional alcoholic who is not a bad person. I'm asking myself, is it the sadness I'm feeling over losing this current relationship, or is it the habitual sadness from childhood? How do I separate the 'sad parts' as 'sad from life situation' part with 'sad from old childhood habit' part?

I appreciate the self-compassion I hear in your email. You understand why that younger you, growing up in an alcoholic home, would have needed to retreat and would have found sadness a safe place to retreat to. At the same time, I would say it in a slightly different way, because the concept of being 'addicted to' sadness, etc. might be keeping the process static, not allowing the movement that is possible.

'Something in you' is holding onto sadness, preferring to retreat into sadness, finding safety in feelings of longing and self-pity. Can you feel the difference when we say it that way? "I am addicted to..." doesn't turn toward the place itself, with an inner relationship of interested curiosity. "Something in me..." invites YOU to turn toward that one, to start listening.

Please don't assume that you know all about why 'something in you' would want to hold onto sadness. "I already know" is another stance that makes change more difficult. You know a lot! But there is more...and by freshly being with the 'something in you' that is holding onto sadness (or whatever words it wants to use for itself) and simply being curious...and then acknowledging what it lets you know...this whole situation can begin to shift.

How to Separate Old Sadness from Fresh Sadness

In the situation you describe, it sounds like the current experience of sadness at losing your relationship is very intermingled with the old sadness. They are not very separate from each other in your experience right now...and that always has to be the starting place: how it is now.

My sense of it is that after you acknowledge both, the older sadness will need the first turn. As you give company to 'something in you holding onto sadness' from earlier times, there will come a sense of a burden lightening, and more space. From there, the current sadness won't be as hard to be with.

I also suspect that there may be some unfinished business with the sadness of losing your young child. Our culture rarely allows people to spend enough time with grieving. You don't have to deliberately go there. Just don't be surprised if that is what comes...and let it be welcome.

DEPRESSION IS A STATE THAT CAN MAKE ONE FEEL LIKE NOT DOING ANYTHING, EVEN FOCUSING. WHAT THEN?

"It is very difficult to Focus if I feel depressed."

It is very difficult to Focus if I feel depressed. I try to Focus with this feeling, but it seems to be even stronger, this bad feeling. You wrote that positive thinking will not work, if we ignore actual feelings. My life theme is depression. I feel often depressed, and I think it is because of this that I cannot do Focusing. What am I missing?

Most of us learned only two ways to be with feelings. We feel them, or we ignore them. If they are bad feelings, ignoring them feels better...but the bad feelings build up, they burst through, and that feels worse. Should we feel or not feel? Either choice has problems.

But there is a third way. Not to feel bad, nor to ignore feeling bad, but to be with the bad feeling. To be with something in me that feels bad, keeping it company.

Now that is really different!

But how do I do it? How can I be with my bad feeling without feeling bad myself?

The answer is simple, but not so easy to do. You need to be Self-in-Presence, your larger Self, larger than the feeling, so you can feel it AND know there is more to you. And it also helps to feel very specifically how it feels in your body right now.

Here is an analogy that may help. Imagine that I ask you to close your eyes, and I hand you a rock. Your task is to feel the rock, sense it exactly: how heavy it is, how smooth, if there is a pointed side, and so on. You are feeling the rock...but YOU are not the rock.

In the same way, you can feel the place in you that is depressed, and yet YOU are not depressed. When you find it in your body, the depressed feeling, let go of the word 'depressed.' No labels, no words for a while. Just sense it, as you might hold in your hand the rock. Sensing how it feels right now, how you would describe it right now. Maybe it's heavy, like a heavy pressure. Now just be with that.

Just Be with What is There

If it's hard to just be with the feeling there — 'heavy pressure' — you could acknowledge something in you that finds it hard. You might find, for example, "It scares me."

"Ah, so it's hard to just be with the heavy pressure because it scares you...something in you feels scared. Maybe you can be with something in you feeling scared. Now you have both — the heavy pressure and something in you feeling scared. YOU are bigger, you are the space that can hold them both."

This bigger 'you' is what we call being Self-in-Presence. Self-in-Presence is something to cultivate; it grows easier and stronger over time.

'Depression' is not simple. It's a whole Tangle of feelings, reactions, frozen places, and protections, and it's different for every person. You might find yourself needing to say Hello to something in you feeling discouraged, something in you feeling doubtful, something in you feeling tired of it all. You might find that this so much easier if you don't have to go through it alone, and having a Focusing partner or professional Focusing Guide or Focusing-oriented therapist would be a gift to yourself.

But the first gift to yourself is to sense into your body until you can say "something in me feels..." and then describe that, using fresh, immediate language. This is a huge step. You might find that even feeling bad can feel, in an odd way, good.

WHEN YOU TRY GETTING TO KNOW WHAT A PART OF YOU IS FEELING, DO YOU FEEL OVERWHELMED AND WONDER WHAT TO DO?

"I tried what you suggested and felt overwhelmed..."

I tried the method you told us about last week, when a part was tired of being tired, or angry about being angry, and so on.

You suggested inviting the part to sense what it is not wanting to happen from being so angry, or from being so tired, etc.

I tried that and felt overwhelmed, nearly faint, like I was hyperventilating. Was I not doing it correctly, or what would you suggest?

DEAR READER:

I knew I left something out of last week's email!

There is an essential step before you make the invitation I talked about, which was:

"I am sensing what it doesn't want to have happen to me."

The essential step is to first be Self-in-Presence. Invitations like that one are a form of deep contact, and they need to come in the context of an inner relationship where you are grounded and strong in your sense of Self. If you aren't, you can get overwhelmed or 'knocked out for the count' by protector parts that don't want you to get overloaded.

Cultivating Self-in-Presence

You can cultivate Self-in-Presence by:

1. Giving yourself experiences of self-care like walking in nature, doing yoga or dancing.

2. Remembering being with mentors and models of Self-in-Presence, when you felt supported and fully accepted.

3. Bringing attention to sensations of lower body support: what your body is touching and supported by.

4. Saying to yourself: "I am the space where all that I feel can be as it is."

You can bring Self-in-Presence into your Focusing by:

1. Saying a gentle "Hello" to what you are feeling.

2. Letting a gentle hand go to the place you are feeling something.

3. Just being with it. Letting it know that you are with it.

4. Saying "Hello" to any other part of you that is feeling scared of this feeling.

5. Allowing all that you feel to be as it is.

6. Letting it know you hear it.

7. When you can be Self-in-Presence with what you are feeling, that creates the conditions for inner invitations that bring forward movement and change.

IS YOUR SADNESS TOO BIG FOR YOU? WOULD YOU RATHER FEEL ANXIOUS THAN SAD?

"Is it possible that very sad feelings start to surface after anxiety gets better?"

I was having frequent anxiety experiences. After some therapy and positive experiences the anxiety is reduced a lot. But now it seems like sadness either got surfaced, or just emerged, to replace the anxiety.

Do you think it's possible that some very sad feelings are sometimes hidden and we are not experiencing them? It's difficult and scary to start Focusing with this, because it's something new, large, it looks like it occupies my whole self.

If I do listen to it attentively and hear what it wants and needs, and I might not be able to change anything, what's the point in asking what the part wants?

DEAR READER:

Yes, absolutely it is possible that feelings, for example very sad feelings, were underneath the anxiety and can now form into something that can be felt because there is a safe enough space for them.

And good for you for noticing that something in you would rather feel anxious than feel this large sad feeling. Might I suggest a small shift in language? (You know me!)

"It's scary to start Focusing with this" becomes "I'm sensing something in me is scared to start Focusing with this." Do you feel that difference? Now you can turn with gentle curiosity toward something in you that is scared, rather than feeling like that scared feeling is you. What we're identified with, we can't give company to.

In the same way, you can feel the place in you that is sad, and yet YOU are not sad. When you find it in your body, the sad feeling, let go of labels. Just sense it. Sensing how it feels right now, how you would describe it right now. Maybe it's heavy, like a heavy pressure. Now just be with that.

"I might not be able to change anything, so what's the point in asking what the part wants?"

With a part that feels sad, I'm not such a big fan of asking "What does it want/ need?" That could too often bring up a part that wants to make this feel better. It's not about making it feel better, but about just being with it, and listening.

This may be — very likely is — something valuable in you that has not been allowed to be. It reminds me of a Focusing session I had soon after my first marriage ended. I found a feeling of sadness about the marriage ending — and I did not want to be feeling that!

Luckily, I was able to acknowledge both the feelings about the marriage ending, and the parts of me not wanting me to feel that way. Then I was able to realize that the sadness was not actually about the marriage ending. It was actually sadness for the parts of me that had been unable to live in that marriage.

I sensed this 'un-lived' side of me, hovering like a ghost in the room with me and my husband all those years. The sadness was for that side of me, the side that could not live in that relationship. This became very precious intention for me...to have a life where all of me could live.

WHAT DOES IT MEAN WHEN YOU CRY SO MUCH WHEN FOCUSING THAT IT LEAVES YOU FEELING LIKE A WRECK?

"Sometimes I cry so much in a Focusing session, I wonder..."

Sometimes I cry so much in a Focusing session I wonder if I was really in Presence. Gendlin said Focusing should feel like fresh air, but today I felt like a wreck after my Focusing. I started off stressed and bothered by several situations in my life, and feel I discovered new territories of pain and distress.

I'm wondering what I'm doing wrong or how I could do Focusing better? Even as I write this I feel the residue of these tears still swimming around in me. I feel sort of washed out, like a shipwreck after a storm.

Throughout most of the session I had a sensation at my throat. It changed and moved about, but I never really understood from its point of view what it was about. I'd really like some help with this.

DEAR READER:

You are so right that Focusing should not leave you feeling like a shipwreck after a storm!

As Barbara McGavin and I have worked with many people over the years, one thing we have noticed is that emotion itself can be problematic — painfully intense, perhaps — from the point of view of something in us. Usually this traces back to early years, to times when the person was very young and had no resources for handling the intensity of an emotion, which would have been a problem in itself. (Think of trying to eat or drink something with too strong a flavor, especially as a child...)

And then on top of that, expression of emotion can bring trouble from our relationships as well. Imagine a child is crying, and a parent threatens, "Shut up or I'll give you something to really cry about!" Now crying — and the emotion underneath it — is doubly scary.

When you say there is a part of you that is tired of the intensity, and another part that wants to get away from people, it makes me wonder if some of this might be going on, that feelings themselves are burdensome and dangerous in relationship to other people.

I suspect that what is coming up in these sessions is something in you that needs your attention, but it doesn't know how to express itself except through crying. It also sounds as if, perhaps, it is not feeling very safe. I say that because the pattern — of feeling a sensation that changes and moves about but never allows us to move into a deep enough contact to sense its emotion — sounds to me like something that is not feeling safe.

It can feel the way it feels as long as it needs to...

In patterns like this, what was missing — and is still missing — is someone offering radical acceptance for the emotions themselves. This calls for being Self-in-Presence!

You might try saying to the one in you who is feeling so much that she is allowed to feel that way, she can feel that way as long as she wants — and you are with her. "I am with you," you can say. Sometimes it helps to let a gentle hand go to your heart or your belly, as you say this.

Then sense if she can feel that you are with her. This might take a while. Another way to do this is to sense what kind of contact she would like from you right now.

In Focusing, contact is first, and contact takes time and patience, especially if safety is an issue. And the time spent making contact pays off, because you increasingly become the safe place where your feelings know they can come, and be accepted. Then they naturally find their own completion.

CAN FOCUSING HELP WHEN YOU HAVE A BIG DECISION BETWEEN TWO CHOICES FOR YOUR FUTURE, AND KEEP HAVING DOUBTS?

I am trying to make a decision about what to study this year. There are many options and directions, and I find myself running from one to another. I have been trying to decide now for more than two months with many Focusing sessions... but always the doubts come back and I can't manage to settle on one option. The doubts tell me I might be missing my true next step and will not be able to grow in my profession as an art therapist.

I would be grateful for your help me with this tormenting situation! I've tried making lists of pros and cons, trying to quiet my mind in order to hear the true answer. Every few days it seems my body is quite clear about a path and then come fears and doubts. I do the process again and come to a different answer...

DEAR READER:

Gene Gendlin always says this about decisions: "If you can't decide between two choices, it's because neither one is right."

Let's pause and take that in...and notice what difference it makes to say this inside: "The reason I can't decide between these choices is that neither one is completely right." Does that bring a deeper breath?

So you might approach the decision this way: For each choice, what is right about this choice, and what is not right?

Listening to doubting parts is also important: not to take their advice but to make sure they feel heard for what they don't want. You can go from not wanting — to wanting — to life energy. ("It doesn't want me to miss my true next step...Ah, it really wants me to take MY true next step...What would it feel like to be taking my true next step?")

It might be that no way, in the real world, is completely right. You might need to decide on an option that doesn't have everything you want. But at least you will do so with open eyes, understanding why you are making that choice, what you are trading. And saying to the doubting parts that you know they are worried...but this is what we are going to do.

"What would it feel like to be taking my true next step?"

This reader tried my advice, and wrote again: "I Focused on the true next step. It felt centered, calm, empowering and strengthening. Nothing on my list suited exactly. How will I truly know, beyond doubt?"

My response:

I don't think it ever works that way: that we know for sure, beyond doubt, before we take a big committed action.

That's why I say (and I have heard Gene Gendlin say): see if you can take a little action. If you are deciding on a course you will take, go and visit the location, talk to the people, ask to talk to others who took the course before. Try it out. Put your body in the situation. It's hard to sense in advance; it's much easier to sense where you are right now.

You may still need to commit without knowing for sure; life is like that. Our bodies don't know the future, only the present. Maybe the doubting parts will relax when you are not asking of yourself that you be sure; just that you are doing the best you can.

DO SOME DECISION-MAKING PROCESSES GO ON TOO LONG? COULD IT BE BETTER JUST TO PUT AN END TO IT BY DECIDING SOMETHING?

"Can it be counterproductive to Focus endlessly on a decision?"

I am in a very rewarding decision process at the moment. I have been in a long distance relationship for three years, and a couple of months ago I moved to my partner's home country to test what it felt like to live together for real. I had been struggling over whether I wanted to live with him and I was hoping to get more clarity by just doing it — moving to live with him.

Now I know more. I find I am not feeling really happy, living here, and we have some difficult relationship issues. A part of me feels really relieved, if I imagine going back home. But still it breaks my heart if I think that our very loving relationship must end.

So both parts seem to be very important.

I've been struggling with this decision for such a long time now, and I am worried that staying much longer in this undecided state is dangerous for my health and my emotional stability. I was hoping that Focusing would help me to find a decision that really feels right for me, but so far, I've just made little steps. Even after five weekends and a lot of inner work, I am not feeling clear.

So my question really is: is it sometimes better to just make a decision if you don't feel that you can stand it any longer? In other words: Can it sometimes — especially because I am a person who reflects and weighs the different possibilities intensively anyway — be counterproductive to Focus endlessly on one's decisions?

In your first sentence you called it "a very rewarding decision process." So at least from one perspective, you are finding this process rich and rewarding! But something in you is ready to stop, ready to just decide something — anything — to end the painful back and forth.

When I work with people on decisions, I find there are typically four parts involved:

1. a part that doesn't want to make the decision;

2. a part that wants to get the decision over, to make it, one way or the other;

3. a part that wants Option A; and

4. a part that wants Option B.

It sounds like you are encountering an intense form of Part #2: "Just get this over with, it's too painful, I'm tired of the struggle, it's hurting my health and my emotional stability to be so undecided."

But I'm not going to tell you that that part of you is any more wise and worth acting on than any other part of you.

It does, however, have something important to tell you (as do all the parts).

My advice would be to BE Self-in-Presence first of all. It sounds like you might be feeling kicked around by this long decision process, tired of it all, and that YOU might want to really acknowledge that part of you that's feeling really tired of the whole thing. And notice if you get at least a breath of relief when you simply acknowledge that much.

What's been a key for me when I make big decisions is to remember: my job is to keep including all of me. I believe that one reason a decision can be hard to make is that we seem to be confronted with options that all feel not completely right.

After all, if any option felt completely right to you, this would not be a big deal, right?

So living with your sweetheart in his country, or not living with him, both feel wrong. Partly right, and partly wrong.

And if that was all there was to it, we might as well flip a coin and get it over with. Luckily, there is more.

Deep Listening from Self-in-Presence Brings Change

We think we're at an impasse, we think we're stuck, because every choice feels partly right and partly wrong.

In my experience, the way through comes when we (Self-in-Presence) take the time to listen deeply to what is UNDER those different choices.

You'd start by saying, "A part of me wants to _____ and another part of me wants to _____." Those are the two sides of the decision, and they can be treated as parts of you that can be sensed in the body.

(No matter what words you use to fill in those blanks, you may find them changing as you do Focusing, so feel free to let them change.)

After acknowledging both, you can sense which one needs the first turn... but assure both that they will get a turn. Then listen for what each one is NOT WANTING to have happen to you (that is its protective tendency) and what it is WANTING you to be able to feel. You might discover, for example, that one side wants you to feel a warm sense of loving connectedness. Perhaps the other side wants you to feel strong and powerful.

You'll almost certainly find that the two wantings are not contradictory. This is an exciting moment. The choices were contradictory, but the wantings are not. I believe a new possibility comes into existence at this moment, and what happens next cannot be predicted. It's a rich and rewarding process indeed!

And what may happen is that a new possibility emerges that wasn't one of the original two. From here, you can't even see it. But from the other side, after holding the listening space, it emerges.

HOW CAN YOU DEAL WITH A STRONG SENSE OF ANXIETY AND FRUSTRATION WITH YOUR LIFE, THAT EVEN WAKES YOU UP AT NIGHT?

"I had a sense of emptiness, this is not going anywhere, nothing is coming."

Frequently, I wake up in the middle of the night with some feeling of anxiety. Sometimes, it is an emotion that, I realize, was repressed during the day, or it could be some deep desire of being able to connect with my son or with other people in general, just a sense of emptiness, etc. This is very unpleasant. And I will remain awake during the rest of the night.

I want to find a purpose for my life...to be able to have a face-to-face conversation with my son...to be able to have intimacy with others, to be able to connect with people in a non-superficial manner...to make a difference in the life of others...not to be so self-centered! A real sense of frustration with all these parts in me.

I have the impression that my 'controlling part' is very active. All these things that I want to happen. I don't know if these two types of issues are related. Should I do some Focusing on these 'I want/I should' feelings? Could Focusing help me at not being so regularly awakened during the night?

DEAR READER:

As you know, Self-in-Presence is a way of being — a quality of energy — where we can make an allowing space for ANY experience we are having. It's a trusting state, and with difficult issues it's not easy at first, but with practice we can cultivate Self-in-Presence more and more. The way to cultivate this way of being is to BE it — for example by saying "Hello" to any part of you that is anxious or untrusting.

If you have a sense of emptiness, just be with that. Emptiness has a quality...there

36

is more there. There is a richness there. It might be that 'emptiness' is a place where something is hiding...and it might be hiding because another part of you is ready to jump on it critically and say, "That's not enough!" That's why it can be so important to acknowledge ALL our parts.

Like this: "I'm saying 'Hello' to a feeling of emptiness in my chest AND I'm saying 'Hello' to something in me that feels impatient with that, wants something to happen."

Do you feel that? If you identified with the impatient part, then no wonder the other part is hiding!

Waking up at night with anxiety

If your 'controlling' parts don't get enough Focusing attention during the day, then they will very likely wake you up at night. This is a type of part that is very anxious, and its anxiety is connected to longing and worries that you will never get what you are longing for.

How would you do Focusing with a part like that? Of course, start with acknowledging it, saying "Hello, I know you're there."

Next, let it know you wonder if it might be worried about something. Let it know you are willing to be its listener and simply hear all that it is worried about. In this case it is probably wanting to tell you what it is worried will never happen, like connecting with your son in a deep way.

It's really great when our process reveals what we are deeply wanting. Let the wanting itself be felt in your body. There is something in you anxious you won't get what you want, AND there is the wanting itself. Perhaps it is the feeling of the wanting that is underneath the emptiness, trying to live. You don't have to know how to fulfill the wanting. You just need to let it live in your body. Then IT will know the way forward.

CAN YOU STILL SAY "SOMETHING IN ME IS WORRIED" IF YOU ARE CONVINCED THERE IS REALLY SOMETHING TO WORRY ABOUT?

"What do you do if you're convinced you can't change?"

At the moment I feel quite desperate, because for a long time I haven't been feeling very successful in my business. Although I have days where I feel optimistic and trustful that things will change, I feel more and more worried that whatever I do, I will never be able to do the things I love and find enough people who appreciate that.

So if I say to myself, "Something in me is worried that I will never have success," it doesn't help me so much because to me, it definitely feels like all of me is worried — and even convinced that things won't change. And the last bit is the worst, to be honest.

I would be so happy to change this conviction because in the beginning of my career I was so enthusiastic and felt much more sure that I could reach what my heart was longing for.

DEAR READER:

Thank you for the opportunity to clarify something important! When we use the words of Presence language: "I'm sensing something in me is worried…" we are not saying that the worry is untrue or unjustified.

You might be really right to be worried about your business. The worry could be a signal from inside you that something needs attention. Not necessarily that you should quit, but maybe you need to spread out to new markets, or get help with your website, or find a second income stream.

When we say, "I'm sensing something in me is worried…" we are not saying it should stop worrying! We are allowing the worried part to form itself as a "something" so we can more easily turn toward it and get to know it better.

When you are in a worried state, all over, it is harder to be a good listener. When you say, "I'm sensing something in me is worried..." and find the worried place inside you — even if it is big — it is easier for you to listen to it, and to sense into it. Maybe there is something that worries it especially. Maybe it is pointing to an area that needs attention. Maybe there is a sense of needing to reach out for business advice. Many possibilities there.

You don't have to disagree with it in order to be Self-in-Presence with it. You don't have to know there is nothing to worry about. That would be untrue. You just need to turn toward it and get curious and interested.

Self-in-Presence is a State of Calm Not-Knowing

My first listening teacher, Les Brunswick, told me that the ideal state of a listener is like a calm pool of water. When you are Self-in-Presence, you are that kind of listener to yourself.

You don't know, one way or another, whether there is something to worry about. You are available to have a look and see what is true. You are available to listen to your inner wisdom. An anxious feeling might be your own body telling you that something needs attention. It's wise to pay attention and then, if necessary, take action.

There might be something real to the worry. There might not. In Self-in-Presence, we don't know one way or the other. We are open, available, interested, curious.

And that will also give you room, dear Reader, to sense freshly what your heart is longing for and to make sure that your heart's desire is included.

DID YOU EVER
HAVE A FEELING
OF HAPPINESS
THAT GOT CRUSHED
BY A VOICE THAT
SAYS, "THAT ISN'T
GOING TO LAST"?

> *"A little voice says, 'You can't be happy. It isn't going to last.'"*

So, something good or exciting etc., happens, and I am happy about it. A little voice, however, says "Oh no you can't be, how long do you think it's going to last, huh?" This dulls my original excitement, and I now have two competing sentiments. So I say "A part of me says I can't happy," AND...and this is where the question comes in. Does 'another part' want to be happy, or, if one senses that it's Self-in-Presence, does one simply say "I" want to be happy?

DEAR READER:

Good for you for noticing that the "How long do you think that's going to last?" voice is something to acknowledge, rather than something to fight with, argue with, or otherwise get entangled with.

That is a type of part that Barbara McGavin and I call a 'protecting/controlling' type. Other people call it the 'Inner Critic' but we prefer a way of talking about it that allows it to change more easily. (Once you call it 'a critic,' how can it be anything else?)

This type of part is driven by worry — sometimes intense worry to the point of anxiety and even panic. If you take a moment, you can almost always sense what it is worried about. In your case, I'd guess it's worried about you being disappointed, if those enjoyable feelings fall flat on you.

(It's ironic and tragic how parts like this often create the very conditions they are worried about!)

This type of part often worries that certain feelings or actions will lead to unwanted emotions. So it seems to be trying to 'control' ("You can't be happy" or "Don't be sad" or "Don't do that") our feelings and actions.

The secret here is not to engage at the level of what it is saying, but rather to acknowledge its underlying worry.

Controlling Part: "You can't be happy, how long do you think that's going to last?"

You: "Ah, Hello. It sounds like you might be worried about something."

Are there two parts: one that says "Don't be happy" and one that wants to be happy?

Actually, I don't think so. The feeling of happy just came to you, like a sunset comes, or a blush. It wasn't a wanting to be happy. You were happy. (*And yes, your whole being can be happy, it doesn't have to be a part of you!*)

When the feeling of happiness came, something in you got scared and reacted. Maybe there was no other part, at that point. Maybe YOU (being Self-in-Presence) kindly and calmly acknowledged that 'controlling' part that got scared. I hope so!

Controlling parts, and actually all our parts, absolutely love for us to be Self-in-Presence. It makes them feel safer! At first, though, they might not trust that you have really shown up. So they need some time and company to get used to you being there. Just listen.

You: "So you're worried I might suffer a big disappointment if I let myself feel too happy. Yes, I really hear, that's what you're not wanting me to go through!"

Hearing what is underneath works its magic, and soon the parts relax and let you go back to being happy!

IS THERE A PART OF YOU THAT SAYS YOU'D BETTER NOT RELAX OR START FEELING TOO GOOD?

> ## *"I have parts that say things like, 'If you relax, you will get hurt.'"*

I have 'parts' that say something like: "If you allow yourself to ____ (relax, feel safe, etc.), eventually something will happen and you won't be prepared to handle/recognize/defend against it, etc., and you will get hurt."

I have worked with these 'parts' during difficult times and during peaceful times but they still persist. I call them 'protector parts.' Is it 'normal' or healthy to have these 'protector parts?' Or are they a part of us that we will continue to need to work with always?

DEAR READER:

If by 'normal' you mean is it typical to have such parts, Yes, absolutely! But if you mean, will they always be there, my answer is No. They can transform and permanently start to express themselves in a more supportive and positive way.

Inner Critics ('Protectors') are always worried about something. It's quite clear what yours are worried about: that you will get hurt.

As often with this type of part, these parts are advising you to suppress emotions. In this case, they want you to suppress emotions of ease and relaxation. Their motivation is anxiety. In my view, 'Protector parts' are parts of us that are quite young, which came into being long ago when you didn't have a strong Self-in-Presence (in yourself or in those around you) to handle tough situations.

They want to sound like wise advisers but they are not: they are kids, home alone. Doing their best...but now, YOU are here.

I would respond to them like this: "Ah! I really hear that you're not wanting me to get hurt. Please tell me more about what you are afraid might happen. I am listening."

"If you relax, you won't be prepared"...is that true?

If you stop a moment, as Self-in-Presence, and ask yourself about this belief that if you relax you won't be prepared, it's pretty clear that it's not true, right? Relaxed alertness is the best position from which to sense and take appropriate actions.

I live in earthquake country, and a few years ago I was often anxious about earthquakes. When I turned toward the anxious part of me, I could sense that it felt it was helping me be prepared, by being anxious. But the truth was I had done nothing to prepare for an earthquake! Being anxious was all I was doing!

After I spent time with the anxious part of me, and really heard its belief that it was helping me to prepare, my feeling shifted. I was more relaxed...and THEN I began to prepare. Now my home and family are more ready for an earthquake in many ways.

But I am not suggesting that you have this discussion with the 'protecting' part of you. Discussing things logically with it will not be the way that it will change.

What I am saying is that, as Self-in-Presence, you hold the understanding that this part of you doesn't know the truth. It is an anxious, hard-working part of you that has done its best to protect you, and your job is to be with it and listen to it at the emotional level, so it feels respected and heard, and its anxiety can ease.

DOES BEING RADICALLY ACCEPTING MEAN YOU TRUST EVERYONE YOU MEET?

"When I feel the bliss of total acceptance, people take advantage of me..."

When I do Inner Relationship Focusing, I start feeling this bliss, this total acceptance not only of my parts and myself, but of others. It's good of course, even great, and I love this feeling. It has even allowed me to make more friends.

But on the other hand, I start feeling more like a child, not seeing anything bad in people. And while it's a popular and pleasant idea to think that all people are good and wish well to each other, it's not the case. These 'protective parts' that close us, that make us less friendly and trusting, aren't that bad, it seems. Since this cute inner child woke up in me and is often taking over, I'm finding myself being hurt and betrayed more.

I do like what this 'child' brings me (that's why it has become so dominant) — I 'feel' more, I can connect to people more, I'm liked more often than when I was closed...but I've also gotten hurt much more, since my curious child started to take on more challenges with people, so I think I need to call another part to help... or to 'wake it up,' or 'bring to awareness' to it, that would appear at appropriate situations.

My child likes to bond, and it is appearing at work, on public transportation, and then feels hurt when it gets mistreated by people who obviously don't care about me or my feelings.

My current goal is both to be able to 'feel' and connect with people, and yet be able to stay strong and not be vulnerable with inappropriate people.

I love your current goal. It's one of my goals, too.

And I'm so glad you wrote, because I can clear up a misunderstanding. Even though I wrote a book called *The Radical Acceptance of Everything*, I am not in favor of trusting people indiscriminately. As you point out, that would not be wise. After all, people that we meet in the world are in all kinds of states. I can believe in their innate goodness, but if they are identified with a part that is impulsive or aggressive, trusting them to take helpful actions is simply not smart.

My book is about radical acceptance of everything in your inner world. And even that doesn't mean allowing every part of you to take every action it wants to take, like chatting with scary strangers on the bus.

I have a question for you. You have a child part that trusts people too much. And you have a protective part that closes you down. But where is Self-in-Presence?

When YOU are Self-in-Presence, you can have your child part and your protective part, but neither one dominates you. Each one can inspire or warn you when necessary. As Self-in-Presence, you have the wider view and the balanced wisdom to discern that one person can be trusted to chat with, and another person you'd better stay away from.

Wise trust comes from the whole self, not from an inner child...

I would disagree with the idea that you have to become your inner child in order to be trusting, and that you have to become your untrusting, closed-off part in order to be safe. Both the ability to trust and the ability to be cautious are qualities that you have available to you, when you are the large Self.

You can even keep feeling blissful, because those enjoyable feelings are still available to you as Self-in-Presence! You'll be able to feel blissful _and_ inwardly strong, as you experience how you are your own inner protector. You can also discern which situations need caution and which situations are appropriate for trust.

53

DO YOU EVER WISH THAT YOU COULD STOP BEING ANGRY SO YOU COULD ENJOY LIFE MORE?

"I was aware I was missing out on a beautiful day and evening with my wife..."

An issue recently came up between myself and a friend, and I grew agitated and angry. She went on vacation. Even though I could see it was probably better to deal with it when she was back in town in three weeks, I sent her an email, she responded, I responded, she responded, and by the third morning I woke up with plenty of anger about it all as an unresolved issue.

It so happened that for the first time in quite a while our kids were out of town, and my wife and I had been looking forward to a relaxing evening, together. But instead I spent the day obsessing about that issue with my friend and by evening I wasn't in a playful mood. I was aware I was missing out on a beautiful day and evening with my wife, just the two of us, and I wanted to be relaxed and open, but I wasn't. I couldn't work up the enthusiasm and missed out on a playful celebration with my wife.

Today I woke up to realize what I've missed, and it is quite disappointing. I'd like this to change. I know other people can set aside a burning issue and enjoy life. For as long as I can remember I have had great difficulty doing this.

DEAR READER:

In reading what you have written here, I am struck by how there seem to be only two choices: be angry, or set aside anger and enjoy life. Without Self-in-Presence and Focusing, those really are the only two choices, and as you've seen, there's not really a choice even there.

When we don't have the ability to BE Self-in-Presence, we are at the mercy of our feelings. They last as long as they last, and we even take actions based on them (like writing an angry email when we know that isn't a good idea), which ends up making them last even longer.

But when we can be Self-in-Presence, being angry is only a part of what we feel, and the part that is angry has company. It has someone (us) who will listen to what it feels so that it can process and change.

It all starts with Presence language. When you hear yourself saying "I am angry," notice that — and try saying instead, "I'm sensing something in me is angry." Then pause and notice if that feels different.

Then try out, "I'm saying 'Hello' to something in me that is angry." You could also sense how it feels in your body.

Here is the next powerful step: Be a listener to that angry part of you. Let it tell you what got it so angry...and don't argue or fix! Just really let it know you hear it. Notice in your body when something that you've heard really makes a difference, bringing a deeper breath or a release of tension. When you've really heard what got it so angry, and it feels you've heard it, it's very likely to let go and not be angry any more, simply because it no longer needs to be.

Actions you now decide to take will come from this larger place, and be calmer, more inclusive, more likely to be welcomed by the other person.

You will also be able to meet the circumstances of your life in the moment, as they are. There is never a need to set anything aside, which doesn't work anyway!

It all starts with those facilitative words: "I am sensing that something in me is _____." I invite you to try them!

IF YOU'RE FILLED WITH SO MUCH ANGER AND RESENTMENT AT SOMEONE CLOSE TO YOU THAT YOU WANT TO HURT THAT PERSON, WHAT CAN YOU DO?

> *"A part of me wanted to hurt my son and didn't want me to do Focusing."*

This weekend I had a hard time with my oldest son, and I found a part that really wanted to hurt him. I managed to just be with that part. It was a lot easier (before I would just freak out when something like that came up) because I have the trust now that when something is ready it will change, and that resisting it will only make it persist.

I was standing in the kitchen this morning and was really identified with my anger and frustration and felt so much resentment. How can I work with this, being so identified that I do not want to go into Focusing, I only want to feel resentment, to justify myself, to think all these yucky things about my son. How would you deal with such a situation?

Yes, there are parts of us that don't want us to do Focusing, because they don't want to stop feeling what they are feeling. Resentment, anger, frustration — those are the kinds of feelings that are often like this.

Maybe these parts of us believe that they will lose something if we do Focusing with them. Maybe they don't know that they will get a chance to tell their story; they will get a chance to pour out what makes them so angry and resentful — to a compassionate, listening ear.

Maybe they are afraid that if you do Focusing with them, you will start to soften, and they don't want that.

And yet at that moment — standing in the kitchen this morning — you were NOT completely identified with those feelings. You did have a larger awareness, enough to know that you were so identified!

How would I deal with it? I would suggest that you start talking (silently) to the parts of you feeling so angry and resentful and frustrated, like this: "Yes, I really hear how angry you are. Of course. No wonder you are angry. No wonder you feel so frustrated. No wonder you don't want to do Focusing. I really hear you just want to feel the resentment. Yes, and I really sense how big that feeling is..."

So you, Self-in-Presence, are there, hearing the feelings as big as they are. There is no hint that they would ever need to be any smaller. They are so big that they don't even want you to do Focusing. Let them know you hear that!

Hear it as big as it is

Once I was listening to two people do a Focusing exchange.

The Focuser said, "This place in my chest is feeling really, really, really sad."

The Companion said back, "You're sensing that place in your chest is really sad."

The Focuser paused, then said, "No, it's really, really, really sad! It needs three 'reallys'!"

And then the two of them laughed. But it was true! Only when the sad place was heard as it was, with all three 'reallys', did it have the space it needed.

We don't make someone feel worse by hearing how they feel exactly as big as it is. And the same is true of our own feelings. When we hear them as big as they are, WE are there, hearing them. That is already a big change. And then the feelings can change as well.

DO YOU FEEL AN INNER URGENCY TO KEEP LISTENING TO ALL THE PARTS OF YOU CLAMORING FOR ATTENTION?

> *"There are so many voices in me that want to to be heard."*

Now that I have experienced that I can really go inside myself and find all kind of answers, it is like I want to do Focusing all the time. And something in me is not feeling good about this, as if it thinks I'll do too much Focusing.

I am having a hard time trying to find a balance because there are so many voices in me that want to be heard, and they kind of scream in desperation. As if they had been closed in a room all my life, and now that I started to open the door, I cannot avoid hearing them or even handle the rush. It feels like I would have to close myself in that room with all of them for a few weeks until every one has been heard to the end. I feel quite exhausted to even just think about this.

I am not quite sure of how to proceed from here and some guidance at this point would be very helpful.

DEAR READER:

As Self-in-Presence you are the space for all the parts...and that means especially the part of you that feels overwhelmed and is afraid that this is all too much. Be sure to give that one a special Hello. It sounds like you are a bit identified with that part, so it needs extra acknowledgement.

Whatever you can do to increase Self-in-Presence is good, like feeling the contact and support beneath you, and saying the words: "I am the space where all of this can be as it is." Feeling the expansion of your breath...relaxing into what feels good in your body, even a little bit.

And when you find a part that is screaming for attention, remember there is nothing you need to do except just say to it, "Wow, I sense how strongly you feel, and how long you have waited." When it knows you are hearing it, just that much, it will relax and allow you to acknowledge something else as well.

I have a secret to tell you, about Self-in-Presence.

You don't have to feel like Self-in-Presence, in order to be Self-in-Presence. You don't have to feel compassionate, or spacious, or friendly to your emotional parts.

(This is good news, because we can't really make ourselves feel anything!)

All you have to do is behave as Self-in-Presence. Act that way.

One of the primary ways to act as Self-in-Presence is to use Presence Language. Just use the language! Make it a kind of discipline, a new habit to get into.

It would sound like this:

"I'm sensing something in me is feeling exhausted just imagining all those parts clamoring for my attention. I'm sensing something in me feeling like I am the one who needs to make them all calm down. And I'm saying "Hello" to that!"

The act of saying this brings a shift. You don't have to wait until you feel it; just be it.

IF YOU HATE YOUR FEELINGS, AND IT FEELS LIKE A LIE TO SAY "SOMETHING IN ME…" CAN YOU STILL DO FOCUSING?

"I have feelings that I'm ashamed to say out loud, and part of me hates them."

Since I started to practice Focusing last year I've been unable to Focus alone. And now I am in a big mess in my life, with feelings that I am ashamed to say out loud, and when I am trying to Focus on those feelings I feel overwhelmed. I can't say they are part of me. I feel the feeling all over me, and if I say "something in me," it's a lie. Part of me hates these feelings. It's hard to deal with them. Maybe you can give me some tips?

Thank you so much for writing. You remind me a lot of myself! I started doing Focusing when I was twenty-two years old, and I had never done anything at all like it before. At first I could feel nothing. I certainly couldn't do Focusing alone.

Then when I started to be able to have feelings, they were all very shameful feelings. I felt like I was turning over rocks that hadn't been moved in a long time, and on the underside of the rocks there were slimy, crawly things that no one would want to see.

Focusing was hard, because every time I did Focusing I was afraid my Focusing partner would look at me with disgust after hearing my feelings.

I remember how difficult it was to get up the courage to say out loud how I felt. But I had no choice. Like inside I was saying, "OK, if you hate me, then you hate me, but I have to say this."

Then I would say it, and I would hear the other person, my Focusing partner, say it back to me in a calm warm voice. It actually didn't bother them! It was a miracle that happened over and over until I finally began to believe (after many months) that maybe my feelings were not so horrible.

In those days we didn't usually say "something in me," and Focusing worked anyway. If you feel that saying "something in me" is a lie, then don't say it. Focusing should be about sensing what is true — what is really so — as you feel it right now.

Focusing is the ultimate in being in touch with reality

Focusing is all about sensing what is actually here, how you are, what you feel, right now. Not just what you think you feel, and certainly not what you should feel, but what you really do feel.

Yes, it will be best if you can find a little distance, or a little difference, from what you feel. Saying "something in me" is one way to do that. Another way to do that is to put a gentle hand on the feeling place in your body.

Gene Gendlin always says that for Focusing we need a friendly attitude. And when people say "What if I can't be friendly?" he replies, "Then see if you can be friendly to that." See if you can be friendly to the not-friendly.

See if you can be friendly to the part of you that hates your feelings. See if you can be friendly to feeling overwhelmed. See if you can be friendly to not wanting to say "something in me." Stay true to what is true. And somewhere in there, Focusing will find you.

FURIOUS, ASHAMED, FEELING DISRESPECTED... HOW DO WE 'UNTANGLE' WHEN FEELINGS SEEM TO REACT & STIMULATE EACH OTHER?

How do we 'untangle' when feelings seem to react & stimulate each other?

I am often furious, very ashamed of it and avoid telling people about it because it has gone on for a long time. I do try Focusing but it only helps momentarily. I can find a kind inner voice for a little while, but again, it doesn't last. I know I need to be patient, but it's challenging.

The fury is, on the surface, with my husband for not clearing up after himself in so many ways, and I feel like a disrespected drudge. He's also very anxious, and I feel I have to make it all right for him. It goes back to my mother's anxiety about me having a disability, and me believing it was my fault, never talked about.

DEAR READER:

It sounds like you have the kind of situation that Barbara McGavin and I would call (in our *Treasure Maps to the Soul* work) a 'Tangle.' It's a situation that affects your whole life, where there are a number of strong emotions and parts of you reacting to other parts of you, and there's no clear way out. In fact you have tried a lot — even Focusing — without getting free of it.

In a Tangle, so many inner parts are reacting to each other that it's really hard to be neutral. One part is furious, another is ashamed. One part is yearning to change, another part is tired of it all. It will probably take some time just to acknowledge all of them.

So let's start by pausing. Find a space and a time when you can be alone and quiet, without interruption, and give that time to yourself. Be comfortable. Maybe have a notebook with you. This is your pause.

Once you get there, you are going to acknowledge all the different parts of you that are warring inside you, like this:

"I'm sensing something in me that is furious at my husband."

"I'm sensing something in me that is ashamed about being furious."

Then take those sentences inside and just check if the words get how it is.

Maybe you'll get, "No, it's not ashamed at being furious, it's ashamed at having a problem that hasn't changed in so long." Just let the words change until they feel right. Your job is to be the listener, to really listen closely to yourself and sense what fits, what gets it just right.

When the words fit exactly, even if they seem awful, you will get a deeper breath.

You are Self-in-Presence; you are the space that holds it all.

When you can acknowledge each of these parts of you, YOU get bigger. YOU are the space that can hold it all.

You said you sometimes find a kind inner voice for a bit but it doesn't last. BE the kind inner voice. And if you can't be kind, that's OK. You can work up to kindness. Start with simply being able to say "Hello."

Fury and anger come from a deep knowing that how it is, is not right. You might want to make a space to honor what you deeply know. In the space of Self-in-Presence, that honoring is more likely to happen.

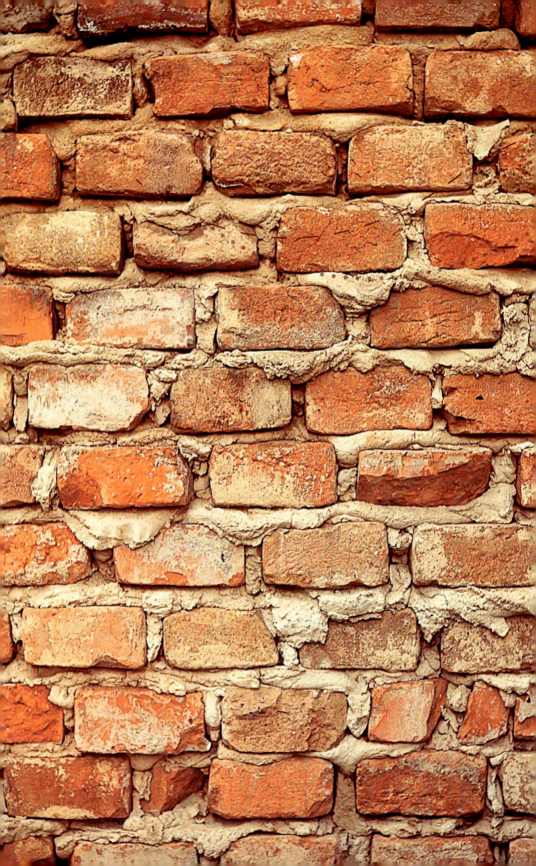

WHAT DO YOU DO IF YOU'RE FEELING 'RESISTANCE' TO GETTING INTO ANYTHING, MAYBE EVEN TO DOING FOCUSING?

"Something in me doesn't want to stir things up or rock the boat."

For the last week and a half, whenever I start to do Focusing or even think about doing Focusing, there is a feeling of resistance, like I don't want to go there, or something in me doesn't want to. Like not wanting to stir things up, or rock the boat. There's a peaceful feeling, or at least it seems that way — and it doesn't want to lose that.

DEAR READER:

Something in us that has 'resistance' — or as I like to re-phrase it, something that "doesn't want to…" — always takes precedence. It is asking for a time-out, it says "wait, not yet, I need more time" — and that request always comes first, before anything else.

One way I like to phrase this is to say, "We cannot move faster than our slowest part."

I don't mean we shouldn't move faster, I mean we CANNOT. We can try…if we're taken over by an impatient part of us, we can try to muscle past the slow, reluctant, "I need more time" parts and try to make something happen.

But that simply doesn't work. We won't get where that part hoped we would. If the slower parts are not respected, they have other methods up their sleeves. We'll find ourselves spacing out, going to sleep, shutting down entirely. For Focusing to work, we HAVE to be Self-in-Presence. There is no other way.

So a part that doesn't want to "go in there" gets to keep its foot on the brake. OK, we say, we won't "go in there" until IT is ready.

What to do in the meantime

So what are you doing, when you don't go faster than the slowest part? Do you just stop Focusing?

No, not at all. You are still Focusing. But you are Focusing with IT.

You don't go past it...you stay with it. You sense how IT feels. You let it tell you or show you what it is worried will happen, if you "go in there." Maybe it wants to let you know it's tired of turmoil. You would let it know you hear that...and listen for more.

Staying with this part, to get to know it better, can actually shift the whole system. We are respecting it, we are not going into the place it doesn't want us to go — but we are also not merging with it.

If you don't turn toward a part like that with awareness, it can keep you away from your process indefinitely, without anything happening at all. But if you respect it, acknowledge it, and stay with it, then ITS process emerging becomes what your whole being was waiting for.

HOW CAN YOU ACTUALLY BE WITH YOUR 'DARKEST PARTS,' IF THEY ARE THE ONES THAT SCARE YOU?

> *"Focusing doesn't work with scary parts because my attention avoids them."*

A READER WRITES:

I've watched your YouTube video where you say it's important to face "our darkest parts." And you've mentioned that even though they're dark (in other words, unpleasant to see and realize they are there), it's important to Focus with them. If these feelings were as easy to deal with as other sensations, no one would have a problem with them! It's easy to be with a 'scared' or 'reluctant' part...but not so much with some 'crazy' part that has 100X intensity when it arises.

The regular way I do Focusing simply doesn't work with scary parts since my attention slips and avoids them...I can't look from some 'Self-in-Presence' perspective and say "it's OK, it's what a part in me has..." The immediate response, at least for me, is automatic, and it's to shift my attention somewhere else, because I naturally don't want to suffer, and that's what finding out that I have these hidden parts causes me.

DEAR READER:

Naturally, you don't want to suffer!

And yet there IS suffering going on, as long as these parts of you are going wild in there. They are suffering...that's pretty obvious from your description of them. And their impact on your life, as long as they are un-contacted and unprocessed, is probably another source of suffering — for you.

I completely agree that it is easier to be with a scared or reluctant part than with a part of us that is full of intensity, that feels crazy or like a dark monster.

So I'd like to tell you about a move that should make it easier to be with even the scariest places inside of you. And that is to turn toward 'something in you' that finds them scary and be with that.

In your case, Reader, that means turning toward something in you that avoids and shifts your attention elsewhere.

"OK, there's the scary part. And now I'm noticing that my attention is slipping away and avoiding. I'm going to acknowledge something in me that wants to avoid the scary part."

So now you are not trying to be with the scary part. Instead, you are being with the part of you that wants to avoid the scary part. You'll probably notice that this one really appreciates your company. And it will have a lot to tell you about what scares it, about the other one. Be the listener! The language that you use will help you remember that these are the feelings of this part of you, not of all of you.

"Yes," you'll say to it, "I really hear that you are scared of it, because you don't know what it is [or whatever it told you]. No wonder you would be scared...Please tell me more."

When this part of you feels heard, you'll very likely feel a body shift that allows the other part, the one called 'scary,' to be calmer and not as scary as before. It's remarkable how that happens!

YOU'RE TRYING TO DO FOCUSING WHEN YOU CAN'T SLEEP BUT **YOUR MIND IS RACING & TOO MUCH IS GOING ON** IN THE BODY. WHAT NOW?

"I get manic/anxious – particularly at night when I can't sleep."

If I do Focusing when I'm anxious, particularly at night when I can't sleep, I do it manically, going from one feeling to the next very quickly. I think there is probably something desperate and very frightened which can't settle and is afraid to slow down or doesn't know how to. I get stuck in a kind of 'thinking' Focusing because there is too much going on in my body, switching from place to place.

The thinking sometimes feels like it doesn't have a container and is afraid of spiraling into strange, mad places. If I do find some relief it's only brief. I know things can seem worse at night, and I do feel saner in the daytime! Do you have any suggestions?

DEAR READER:

My first suggestion would be, slow down! I do hear that something in you is afraid to slow down, but that doesn't mean you can't go slower AND acknowledge the part of you that finds it scary to go slower.

As for how to slow down, I have a number of suggestions:

First: Speak out loud. This is a huge help when doing any Focusing alone. Speaking out loud will automatically slow down your process to the speed of your speaking voice. (As you know, the mind can go much faster than that, and along half a dozen pathways at once!)

Second: Use Presence language. "I am sensing something in me feeling…" It may sound odd at first and a bit of a formula, but I predict you'll find it SO helpful to speak this way. Just try, and I think you'll feel the benefits immediately.

Third: Acknowledge especially the parts of you that feel like they are in the way of this process working. Like this: "I'm sensing something in me that can't settle and is afraid to slow down. I'm saying 'Hello' to that." Then take time to feel the "Hello" being received. It may also help to put a gentle hand on the place where you are feeling this. Placing the hand is a really nice thing to do because it reminds you to be kind to what you are feeling.

"There's so much going on in my body..."

It sounds like you are feeling a bit 'at the mercy' of your body feelings. That's one of the most difficult times, when it feels like our emotions and anxieties are bigger than we are.

The solution is to get bigger...and that's why I developed the five-part process called **Get Bigger Than What's Bugging You** that includes saying "Hello" and the touch of the gentle hand. It's free and comes as a five-day e-course. You'll get one email a day for five days. You can visit our website at: www.focusingresources. com/getbigger to sign up.

The trick is to actually do these things! When you're lying in bed at night feeling overwhelmed you may have fewer resources than usual. So sit up! The act of intention involved will remind you that YOU are doing something.

Remember: doing Focusing is a deliberate action. Just lying down and letting your body feelings run riot...well, I wouldn't call that Focusing, would you? When you do Focusing, you're deliberately pausing, deliberately bringing awareness to how you feel with an open, kind curiosity.

If you do that, I predict you soon will be finding your thoughts slowing down and your breathing getting deeper and calmer, as the feelings and parts inside you begin to trust that you are there.

WHEN THE TRIGGER FOR PAINFUL FEELINGS IS SOMETHING FROM CHILDHOOD, IS THERE A SPECIAL WAY TO HANDLE THAT IN FOCUSING?

"When the trigger is from my childhood, it causes me anxiety all day long."

I have a question. When I Focus I start to see the source of the 'felt sense,' what happened to make this feel that way. I realize the 'trigger' is because of something from my childhood. I stay with it and put a hand on it. I sometimes feel the 'release' or 'calm' but it keeps coming back in my mind throughout the day and causes me anxiety all day long. Also I feel it is difficult for me to separate myself from the feeling. Is this all 'normal' or am I doing something wrong?

Well, what you're going through is normal in the sense that many people experience it. But I don't think it's necessary; I think I can help. Glad you wrote!

It's very natural to discover that something that is bothering us today has its source in childhood. In my experience there is a way of framing this that makes the healing process more supported and less anxiety-producing.

First, I like to use the word 'something' for my inner experience. This allows me to have a relationship with it in the present. I would say, "I am sensing something in my belly that is scared." (And not, for example, "There is fear in my belly.")

Then I would put my hand on it gently. (Just as you did, Reader.) Along with putting my hand on it, I would say, "I know you're there, I am with you, I am listening." So I have a gentle relationship of listening with this something inside me.

Now, if I start having memories from my childhood, I understand that this 'something' in me is showing me those scenes. It (or she, as I might call her) is showing me what she went through. This is important because at the time, there would have been no one to receive her and her feelings compassionately with no judgment.

I stay in the listening mode and I keep saying, "I hear you, I see you, yes, that was hard, what you went through." When she has shown me what she really wanted me to see about how it was back then, I get a deep breath of relief.

Even after the Focusing session is over

At the end of such a Focusing session, I will say to this 'something' that I am with: "I'm sensing how you would like me to be with you, even after the session is over."

In other words, the relationship continues. I continue to be the strong, compassionate Self-in-Presence, giving an allowing space and tender company to this part of me that is carrying the pain of the past. I am grateful that it came, and I know there is a healing process going on that requires ME to be here, BEING WITH this part of me. Throughout the day, if I sense it calling to me (and that might be signaled by an anxious feeling) I will turn toward it and offer it a gentle touch of my hand, and a kindly, "Yes, I know you're there."

Maybe as I fall asleep that night, I will whisper to that part of me that I am with it, I am listening.

I hope it's clear that seeing this process as a relationship of caring and support with a part of us that is carrying suffering from the past is quite empowering and healing.

If you need help in separating from feelings, you might want to take my free e-course, **Get Bigger Than What's Bugging You** (see p. 85). It can really help with being with feelings without getting taken over by them.

WHEN YOU FEEL SO ANGRY YOU'D LIKE TO HIT & KICK & SMASH SOMETHING, IS THERE A SAFE WAY TO DO FOCUSING WITH THAT?

"Is there a safe way to put Focusing attention on huge anger?"

I was fired from the job I'd had for over 30 years. I've suffered a great financial loss, because of the reduction in the pension I've worked for all these years. As great a loss as that is, the emotional damage from this action seems far greater and even less manageable.

One place where I falter is when the anger gets so big it seems like it could take over. I've sensed a desire to break things, say things I'd regret, throw things, or strike out in some way. What if I hurt someone else? At those moments, I've slammed the lid down on that anger and held it off.

Is there a safe way — safe for me, safe for my listener — to put attention on something in me that is hugely angry with something that has happened to me? That wants to lash out at the people who did the damage? That wants to say all the terrible things that boil up inside from what seems at times like a full chorus of angry voices?

DEAR READER:

Anger usually comes from a deep knowing that what happened was WRONG. It often has to do with 'fair' and 'unfair,' with 'justice' and 'injustice.' It sounds like something in you is deeply feeling the wrongness, the unfairness, and the injustice of what happened to you. Does that fit?

And I'm also hearing that there is another something in you that feels unsafe in the presence of that very angry part. Afraid that the angry part could take over, and that's the part that slams the lid on.

Notice that what that literally means is that something in you is afraid that YOU will not be able to be Self-in-Presence and hold the space for the part that is so angry. That part too needs to be acknowledged.

What does it look like and sound like, when a person is holding Self-in-Presence with a part of them that is SO angry?

You'd see and hear a person who is careful to use Presence language. Instead of "I am angry," that person would say, "I am sensing something in me is angry." The voice doesn't have to be quiet and sweet. That wouldn't be true to the feeling! But there is a clear difference between the 'I' of Self-in-Presence and the 'something' that is so angry.

"I'm letting it know I really hear how much wants to smash and kick."

Instead of saying "I want to kick out and smash things," be sure to say, "IT wants to kick out and smash things." Taking care with language like this can be a powerful support to staying Self-in-Presence.

And then say to it, with strength in your voice, "I really hear HOW MUCH you want to kick out and smash things."

And then listen to what is UNDER the impulse to kick and smash. What really brings transformation is never the discussion about what action to take. Rather, it is hearing and acknowledging what drives the impulse to action.

Underneath its anger there will be something more...and the safety for hearing that comes from YOU being there, steady and calm, holding the part that is angry right now so that it really knows YOU are there.

WHAT IF YOU ARE TAKEN OVER BY PAINFUL STATES OF RAGE THAT FEEL UNCOMFORTABLE AND DON'T FEEL LIKE "SOMETHING IN ME?"

> { *"I get these surges of anger, out of nowhere."* }

A READER WRITES:

I get these surges of anger, out of nowhere. I can't say that they are something in me, or somewhere in me. I find myself abruptly going from one annoying thing to another and suddenly I'm plunged into a painful state of rage, horribly uncomfortable — it isn't enjoyable rage. I don't feel strong and full with it — it is a sort of rage and weakness and impotence all at once, and I am in it, I'm not outside it. It isn't 'something in me' — not to me, no, it feels like ALL of me. In that moment, I'm just all anger.

How do I deal with sudden surges of engulfing anger, anger that I don't enjoy feeling, that makes me feel really uncomfortable. I guess, for one thing, there must be a sense that my anger is not OK — or dangerous. Yes, that rings a bell — when I was an angry boy my father convinced me that if I went on showing temper he could and would kill me. A sense of sorrow and shame about that...

DEAR READER:

It's beautiful how, even while writing to me, you got a shift in your understanding of the part of you that doesn't like the angry part. No wonder, if your father threatened your life if you showed temper, anger would feel dangerous even now.

So there is something in you that finds the angry, rageful feelings dangerous to allow, dangerous to feel. You are beginning to understand why it feels that way, so you can speak compassionately to this part of you — we can call it the part that is scared of the angry part.

You can be present for both — you can be the space where both are there: something feeling rage and something afraid of that.

Because YOU are Self-in-Presence, this makes your inner world a safer place for both emotional parts...and now they can each be in process, and the body's own change can begin to emerge.

Why a part of you might take over completely and refuse to be called "something in me"

I suspect you had been identified with the part scared of the rageful part. I can hear this in your language, when you say things like, "Anger that I don't enjoy feeling, that makes me horribly uncomfortable."

If you're identified with a part that doesn't like a rageful part, and try to use language like 'something in me,' of course the rageful part will refuse that language. It is quite sensitive, and it can tell that the language is being used to try to control it rather than as a way to get to know it better.

These two parts have been in a life-and-death struggle, what Barbara McGavin and I call a 'Tangle.' The rageful part has a part of your unlived life, waiting to live forward, as well as painful emotions needing to complete. The part scared of the rageful part and trying to control it is convinced that even feeling it can put your life in danger. This intensity of this struggle can feel quite painful in itself. And since each of these parts is trying to save your life, neither one is going to give up.

Only one thing can bring relief and the possibility of fresh air: being Self-in-Presence, holding the parts in acceptance for how they are. Not taking sides... recognizing that each side in this inner war has been trying to protect you and trying to hold onto your integrity. Acknowledging this to each of them.

When you can do that, then something new can happen: insight, fresh feelings, relief, new possibilities.

HOW CAN FOCUSING BRING A SHIFT WITH THE ISSUE OF UNFULFILLED DESIRE?

"How do I work with Unfulfilled Desire?"

I've seen references to Unfulfilled Desire in your work on blocks, but no detail about it or about how to work with it. Unfulfilled Desire characterizes my life in all areas, and I'm wondering if you could say something about it and how working with it differs from working with blocks.

DEAR READER:

In Unfulfilled Desire, there is a war between the part of us that holds onto the desire (even though it is unfulfilled) and the part of us that wants us to let go of the desire.

Unfulfilled desire is painful — often very painful. From the point of view of the one part, the way to feel less pain is to let go of the desire. "Be realistic," it says. "Face the facts. Settle for something easier to get." It may even take on a critical tone and tell us there is something wrong with us, so we will never get what we want. Its underlying purpose for these nasty remarks, however, is oddly benevolent: it wants us to give up so we aren't tormented by desire any longer.

And then there is the part that holds onto the desire. It doesn't care if the desired object, person, or state seems unobtainable, it WANTS it...and it knows that settling for something less will not satisfy it.

This is a war between parts that itself is painful and goes to the very nature of what is real and what is possible.

So how do we work with Unfulfilled Desire?

To work with Unfulfilled Desire we need Self-in-Presence, lots and lots of it! We need to acknowledge, over and over, "Something in me desires or longs for..." AND "Something in me says I should give up or settle..." and keep doing that as often as necessary as we (probably) keep slipping into identification with one part or the other.

From the position of Self-in-Presence we will be turning toward first one part, then the other, to compassionately get to know what is under the urgency of its position. Ultimately we will hear — and feel — what each part is wanting us to be able to feel.

After years of longing for a particular person for my life partner, and doing a lot of Focusing with the two sides, the longing finally shifted to a longing for a particular KIND of person. In session after session I felt the longed-for body feeling: supported, met, both strong and vulnerable. Within a few more months I had met him, and we are still happily partnered after fourteen years.

WHAT IF YOU GET SUCH STRONG FEELINGS WHEN YOU 'FALL IN LOVE' THAT YOU AVOID ANYONE YOU'RE ATTRACTED TO?

"When I'm attracted to a man, the feelings are so overwhelming..."

When I'm attracted to a man, my feelings are so overwhelming that they paralyze me. It happens when I fall in love, or have a crush, or just like someone. That's why I always date only those people I don't have strong feelings for, just who I'm comfortable with. But I'd like to be able to date a man I'm attracted to! I've heard from many people that it's normal to have overwhelming feelings, but I'm thinking maybe mine are stronger, because when I feel I'm falling for someone I'm sabotaging them somehow. I indirectly reject a guy, hoping he'd understand and pursue me further...but they probably think I'm not interested at all by the indifferent way I act, and back off.

DEAR READER:

It certainly sounds like there are parts involved! I would say there is a part of you that falls in love and has the strong feelings for the person, and another part of you that paralyzes you and keeps you away from the person.

Strong feelings of love and longing are an indication that a very young part is involved. This is probably a part that is searching for a 'savior' — a person who will save it, usually by loving it unconditionally.

This kind of part (called a 'Small One') holds a lot of life energy and knows something about what you need to be whole and complete. But without Self-in-Presence, this part can take over your body and lead you to take actions that don't carry your life forward.

Another part of you knows this and takes on the job of suppressing the feelings and de-railing the actions of the Small One. This other part is extremely worried that an out-of-control Small One will lead to great trouble and danger. It could be right about that, but the way it suppresses and uses shaming to control other parts will also not carry life forward.

Why Self-in-Presence is So Important

Without Self-in-Presence, this struggle between parts is endless. None of them has a way out. They are driven by powerful unmet needs and they are not going to give up their positions, which they hold ultimately to save YOU.

With Self-in-Presence, the struggle can start to unwind. YOU are there, compassionately acknowledging each one of them.

You say to the Small One: "Yes, I really sense how much you long for someone to see you completely and adore you totally." You say to the other part: "Yes, I really sense how worried you are that the strong feelings will get out of control and lead to danger." And then listen. Each one has more it wants to tell and show you.

You may want to do this work with someone else, because it can be hard to hold Self-in-Presence alone with such powerful and ancient feelings. AND it can be so releasing when the parts finally take in that YOU are there, and the life-forward energy that has been bound in this struggle begins to take the form that it has always truly needed… and your relationships can be between two real people!

ARE YOU JUST ATTRACTED TO THE PEOPLE WHO AREN'T ATTRACTED TO YOU? WHAT'S THAT ALL ABOUT?

"I fall for the uninterested guys, and I'm not interested in the nice ones…"

The men who I fall in love with actually seem to be wrong for me; they are not even interested in me seriously.

I seem to choose wrong people, or get scared and even repulsed by 'respectful, nice, good-looking men' who sincerely seem to be interested in me. My close girlfriend has exactly the same story — she rejects perfectly normal and smart men, and also falls for 'cool and good-looking,' but who are only interested in flirting.

As an example, when this guy asked me out, and we were on a date, his niceness was scaring me. He gave me flowers, was opening doors for me, was very respectful, but inside I got a familiar uneasy feeling I have gotten before. One part is afraid that now I can't be myself and have to act nicely. It's afraid that if I say something straightforward, he'd reject me.

DEAR READER:

My own take on it is that you are facing the most fundamental issue of being a social human: Can I be me and still be with you? Pretty much all of us came from childhoods where that wasn't the case, we couldn't be fully ourselves AND be accepted by those around us. Some part of us at least was unacceptable, and probably we decided to hide it or exile that part of us completely.

And maybe we even came to believe that it's true: I can't both be myself AND be in a relationship. That presents a dilemma. As soon as a real relationship looms close, my parts get in a panic. "Am I going to lose myself?" Sometimes the longing for closeness is so great that we throw our own selves to the wind. And sometimes we keep our own integrity and reject relationships.

Falling for Unavailable People — The Perfect Solution

If you are still stuck with this unexamined belief — that you can't both be yourself AND have a real connection with another person — getting really close to someone brings on panic. But we long for closeness. So what people often do — I know I have — is to be attracted to people who are 'safe' somehow — far away, or unavailable for some reason, or just not that interested in us.

We get to have those yummy feelings of love and attraction, and longing. Longing might be painful but it also makes us feel very alive. And at the same time we are safe from the challenges of real connection, where we might need to stand up for our own point of view while making room for the other.

Another thing about longing: It echoes back to childhood again, where we may have felt longing for more connection and tenderness than we received from our parents. The longing that is here now links back to that older longing, and gets much of its poignancy from there.

And a way through all this is with Focusing! Give yourself time to be with the parts that get scared of real connection and the parts that long for something far away and impossible...and be the calm Self who can really hear them. They can and will change to something more free and more in the present, able to balance integrity and connection.

WHAT IF YOU HAVE A PART THAT IS 'PROTECTING' YOU BY PREVENTING YOU FROM GOING AFTER WHAT YOU WANT?

"He will be appalled when he gets to know me better..."

For quite some time, I have been aware of at least two parts: One is longing for a loving relationship and the other one wants to avoid getting to know someone because it is ashamed of very many things, e.g. my looks, way of life, etc. Practically everything.

This part says, "He thinks I am great but I am not. He will be appalled when he gets to know me better." It wants to save me from the pain of being rejected instead of being loved. And this part is absolutely convinced that this will happen and it feels real terror as soon as I like someone. I have listened to it quite often but have not experienced any change, yet.

Do you have an advice for this? This part seems to stem from my childhood (it showed me scenes from my childhood), but also seems to have been reinforced in recent years and there really is this intense emotional quality of being ashamed and wanting to run away and hide.

P.S. I think a loving relationship is a human need so I am not really unbiased with regard to this subject, but I do try not to press this part and I believe I am Self-in-Presence when I listen to it.

This is a tough one! And I really appreciate how much you have done to make a safe inner space for this part of you to be heard...by not pressing it, by doing your best to listen as Self-in-Presence.

You say you have listened to it quite often but have not experienced any change yet.

So…I am wondering about what counts as 'change.' If change means that you are in a fulfilling love relationship already, then no, that change hasn't come yet. But have you perhaps experienced a 'micro change'? That would happen if the part feels so understood by you, that you experience a sigh of relief moving through your body. That much change should have happened. And if it didn't, it means that the listening-to-it needs to deepen and get more precise. (If it did, we can expect a series of those, in a number of sessions, to add up over time to bigger changes in action and belief.)

"I'm letting it know it can be the way it is for as long as it needs…"

Clearly this kind of part, that feels so deeply ashamed of who you are that it actually believes you cannot be loved, must spring from early trauma. Events that lead to the belief that we cannot be loved are traumatic events…since being loved is one of the most basic of human needs. Your whole body has known all along that something 'wrong' happened here.

The place where the wounding lives needs your company. It needs you to be Self-in-Presence: calm, centered, compassionate, steady, and warm. It needs you to say to it that it can be the way it is, as long as it needs to be…and you will be with it. Perhaps bringing to it a gentle hand will emphasize the tender quality of your company.

From there, I'd recommend sensing and describing exactly how it feels. Let it be as it is, and sense how it is. The more precise you can be in 'getting' it, the likelier will be those deep whole-body breaths that signal that something needed has occurred.

Being the Self who can give compassion to this part for what it went through adds to your strength, resilience, and resourcefulness. And you can feel that, too.

WHAT IF YOUR 'WANTING' FEELS MORE LIKE A DESPERATE DEMANDING?

"The result must look like this!"

I did a Focusing exercise that invited us to sense the 'wanting.' In my Focusing, I noticed an initial wanting that I experienced as frantic, demanding, and "the result must look like this" energy. This wanting feels familiar because I have wanted (with this type of energy) the situation to change for a long time.

Then I came to a different kind of wanting, one that was deeper, calmer, more open, and willing not to know exactly what change would look like.

The two experiences of wanting feel so different that the same word 'wanting' feels misleading. I wonder if different words might be useful or perhaps different descriptors, such as frantic wanting vs. deep wanting.

DEAR READER:

What I love about language is that it is so adaptable! It sounds like you are well on your way to describing a very important distinction.

To me what you have described is the difference between the wanting of a part (or Partial-Self) and the wanting of one's whole self (or Self-in-Presence).

"What I want" can feel so many different ways, including frantic or deep, demanding or open, desperate or relaxed. The important thing is to sense the quality of the wanting, whatever it is.

And then — I love this — even the wanting that has a desperate, frantic, "the result must look like this" quality about it can yield a positive next step. It doesn't have to stop feeling how it feels. It just needs for YOU to be with it with compassion and curiosity.

How to invite the next step when there is a desperate wanting.

First, use Presence language. "I am sensing something in me really wants _____ and feels quite desperate and frantic about it."

Acknowledge. "I am letting it know I know it's there."

Invite what it is not-wanting. (Really? – Yes, if there is a 'wanting' that is desperate and frantic, it is surely not wanting something as well.)

"I am inviting it to let me know what it is not wanting to happen if I don't get what it wants."

And then, whatever comes next, let it know you hear it. You'll probably notice that when this part of you experiences that you are listening to it respectfully, it's very likely to calm down.

Very likely you'll soon start to sense the other kind of wanting emerging from this very same place...like a wanting for you to have connection, warmth, peace...as you feel those feelings in your body right now. Enjoy!

CAN WE EXPECT FOCUSING TO HELP WITH GRIEF, LOSS AND HEARTBREAK? DON'T WE JUST NEED TIME TO GET OVER IT?

> *"No insight has been able to transform these painful feelings."*

A READER WRITES:

A relationship has ended recently, and I've been suffering a great deal. Feelings of loss and hurt seem to be screaming for my attention.

I'm finding that Focusing in this area has value (self-awareness, insights, etc...) but the transformational element of Focusing seems to be limited in this realm of grief and loss. No insight has yet been able to transform these painful feelings of loss that I'm experiencing.

The lyric may be true that, "When you got a heartache, there ain't nothing you can do." I can be Self-in-Presence with this heartache, but there are no guarantees of shifts or transformations. I need help understanding what I can reasonably expect from this practice, or better yet, what is an unreasonable expectation.

DEAR READER:

I would agree that grief and loss have an organic quality of 'this needs to happen' and 'this cannot be rushed.' The feelings of grief have their own timing.

But we can make the time take longer than it needs to in two ways:

1. By trying not to feel so bad. Or,

2. By getting identified with the bad feeling.

There is something else that can happen when YOU — as Self-in-Presence — can BE WITH the feelings of grief and hurt. It's not that they won't hurt. It's that they will have company. That's a big thing — to be giving a comforting quality of presence to yourself, to be saying to the something(s) in you that are feeling hurt and grief, "Yes, I am with you."

Yet even that is not the whole gift that Focusing can bring.

"What is it about me that this hurts in just this way..."

The rest of what Focusing can bring is a further process that has a quality something like, "What is it about me that this hurts me in just this way...?"

There IS something that makes this hurt exactly THIS hurt and not another hurt.

Maybe it's that...you were imagining your future with her in a certain way. Or...she was exactly the person you always wanted. Or...she was not the person you always wanted but you went to all the work of making that be okay anyway, and THEN the relationship ended.

And so on. It will be unique to you.

All those examples, as I write them, seem to me more logical and more cognitive than what the process is actually going to feel like, when you get in there and sense what it is about THIS and about YOU that this hurts in just THIS way. It will be fuzzy and unclear and at first really hard to articulate and all you will know is that there is something there. And then you spend time with it, and you get something, but it makes no difference in your body, and that's how you know that however true that was, it isn't all of it.

And finally you get the one that gives you a big deep breath — "Ah, that's what it is!" — and then even though nothing has changed and she is still gone, you feel mysteriously lighter.

AND you will still feel sadness and loss, but not quite to the same degree. As the guy says, pain is inevitable but suffering is not.

WHAT CAN YOU DO WHEN A PART OF YOU BECOMES ASHAMED SO QUICKLY AND DEEPLY THAT YOU CAN'T FIND SELF-IN-PRESENCE?

A READER WRITES:

Here's what happens. Something comes up that feels very very anxious. The moment I contact it in Focusing, something else comes that judges the anxious one as bad, stupid, childish and a burden to everyone. Then it quickly goes to deep shame. I know the judging, ashamed part is worried, but I can't go there easily — the shame is so, so strong. I feel engulfed by it. What do I do to find Self-in-Presence?

DEAR READER:

You describe a classic reaction pattern...an inner war where neither side can allow space to the other. And you're absolutely right that this process needs for you to be Self-in-Presence above all.

Remember that Self-in-Presence is you, the real you, the natural state of your Self. So it's not something you have to find, but something to be, to cultivate.

And I would invite you also to remember that in any difficult area of life, it is hard to be Self-in-Presence. That's really what defines it as a difficult area! So it's understandable — we could even say "normal" — that Self-in-Presence is hard to find in a situation like the one you describe.

Perhaps the first acknowledgment (which I learned from Barbara McGavin) is this one: "I'm really sensing how hard it is to be Self-in-Presence right now." When you do that, you are at least a little bit closer, aren't you?

Then you might say to the part that is ashamed, "I really really sense how deeply ashamed you feel, how you feel that you want to sink into the ground and disappear and never be seen again." (I'm just guessing. You would say to it what you sense from it about how it is feeling.) The important thing here is that YOU (Self-in-Presence) are sensing exactly how it is for IT, and letting it know you sense it — how it feels, how strongly it feels, as strongly as it feels that way.

What happens when you do this is that you start to embody the fearlessness of Self-in-Presence. You are willing and able to sense and be with how this ashamed part of you is, exactly as it is. IT may be ashamed, but YOU are not. You are its listener, giving it empathy for how ashamed it is.

And then there's the anxious part...

You were also speaking of another part of you, one that feels very anxious. You were saying that even a touch of awareness on that part, in a Focusing session, brings up another part of you that judges it harshly.

If your emphasis is on how much it is a burden to everyone, it's not surprising that your encounters with it bring up instant judgment. It's hard to be Self-in-Presence with a part that is experienced as being so burdensome and limiting.

But from its point of view, it has some good reason to be anxious. It isn't trying to be a burden. That's how it is seen by others, it sounds like, and by a part of you.

Listening as Self-in-Presence you will be able to give it a chance to tell you what gets it so anxious, and what it is not wanting to happen to you. That alone is likely to bring some relief.

IF YOU HAVE A CORE BELIEF THAT YOU'RE USELESS, DOES IT DO ANY GOOD TO FEEL THE FEELINGS AROUND THAT?

> *"It's a part that says 'I'm no good, useless, bad, a failure, crap."*

What comes up regularly is a part that says, "I'm no good, useless, bad, a failure, crap." It can come up regardless of anything I am or am not doing in the world — more like a core belief that gets activated and with it are all sorts of really uncomfortable feelings — shame, sobbing, rage, despair/helplessness, etc. At such times, it's quite hard to operate in the world. I understand the roots will be from childhood and that I must have adopted and absorbed this belief as the best way to survive at the time.

However, even though I realize this, I find it very hard to dis-identify from this wounded part — it feels 'true' even if another part of me can reason with it and say otherwise, and say that it is just a belief. I guess the belief and messages are coming from a critical part of me, though I am more merged with the part experiencing the pain.

Sometimes I am concerned that if I Focus too much on the feelings — acknowledging them and sensing what they are, etc. — that can just take me deeper into pain. But ignoring them or denying them doesn't help either, of course. I find it hard to see where the 'gold' is in all this — the sense of forward movement. It's a bit like I'm stuck in a loop (a part of me is stuck in a loop?) at these times.

The first thing I would suggest is to avoid the concept of 'core belief.' I'm not saying it isn't true or valid, but in my experience, the inner discussion about beliefs doesn't go anywhere. It's like 'referred pain.' It's not where the real material is.

One part says, "I'm useless," and another part says, "I know that isn't true," but knowing it isn't true doesn't change anything...and as you yourself put it, there is a loop here we can just stay stuck in.

What is under the loop is a fundamental struggle: There is pain, and there is not wanting to feel pain. The bigger the pain, the more the desperation of the part of you that doesn't want you to have to feel it. And yes, this is all about the past, all about a time when the pain of some kind of trauma (lack of what you needed to thrive) was really too much for the little one that you were.

What needs to happen is what couldn't happen then

What was missing back then was Self-in-Presence — both in you and in the caregivers around you. Little kids need their caregivers to be gentle and strong, and help them contain hard feelings and get through them. Without that, the inner wounded parts stay frozen in time, ready to get triggered by almost nothing and to emerge in a way that feels like there's no way to help.

You need to BE that nurturing Presence, strong and gentle to your own feelings. There's no need to say things like, "It will be all right." Who knows that anyway? Just be a listener. "Ah, THAT'S how bad it feels!" And it's not just how bad it feels, but also how bad it felt. It is showing you how it was, back then. It needs to show you it was this bad, and it needs you to be a compassionate witness.

I'm not saying you have to remember what happened. Everything you need to know is being shown by the feelings themselves. "That's how bad it feels/felt." The feelings can be as precise as they need to be. Maybe there's nausea, for example. Or a sense of helplessness. It is showing you that.

The 'gold' in it is that so much of yourself and your energy has been bound up in holding this back, that when you finally turn toward it simply to feel it, you get yourself back as well.

WHEN WE HAVE NEGATIVE IMAGES INSIDE PASSED ON TO US FROM CRITICAL PARENTS, WHAT CAN WE DO TO GET FREE OF THEM?

I grew up with a very critical mother, so during my childhood I took in an extremely bad self image. Today my life is good in many ways. But on occasion when I Focus on a stressful situation, an image of a well-known tyrant appears, an infamous person. He is behind bars and staring at me, and when, with great difficulty, I acknowledge him and ask him if he has anything that he would like to share with me, he tells me that he wants me to know that I am a bad person. I am not sure how to use Presence in such a negative situation.

DEAR READER:

I wouldn't ask a critical, negative tyrant if he has anything he wants to share with me! That's way too open-ended an invitation.

Yes, I would say "Hello." But what comes after "Hello" would not be, "Is there anything you want to share with me?" First, we need to facilitate a shift in point of view and quality of attention.

In this case, because the image you are seeing is of a historical person, I would suggest you use these words: "Something in me shows me an image of _____."

Then say "Hello," not to the tyrant himself, but to the part of you that shows you the image of the tyrant.

Next, say to THAT part, "You must be quite worried about something." This is the key. Critical parts of us are worried, and they are almost always telling us (literally) what they are worried about.

It sounds like this part of you is worried that you might be a bad person. Since you grew up with a very critical mother, we don't have very far to look for the source of this worry.

Harshly Critical Parents & the Stopped Process That Results

We're born with the readiness to be accepted completely and lovingly for exactly who and what we are. If that doesn't happen, part of our life energy gets stopped. When the criticism from a parent is severe, this is a very difficult situation for a little one. It can feel life-threatening to be so harshly criticized by someone upon whom you depend for everything.

Our Partial-Selves are always trying to save our lives. One strategy they attempt is to take sides with the persecutor. "If I can be as critical of myself as my mother is, maybe my mother will appreciate that I am on her side...and maybe I can even perfect myself enough so that she will love me."

From the present time, from Self-in-Presence, it is a transformative and healing process to be understanding and compassionate toward the very parts of us that seem harshest to us. They are driven by fear and worry, and are trying to save us from a worse fate. They are doing their best.

Stopped process can resume again. In the atmosphere of compassion from Self-in-Presence, what was missing can now be filled in. It is never too late.

WHAT IF A PART OF YOU IS SURE YOU'RE GOING TO MAKE A COLOSSALLY BAD DECISION, JUST LIKE YOU HAVE IN THE PAST?

> *"The voice says, 'Look at the mess you've made of all those other decisions!'"*

My Focusing question has to do with really big decisions. Something in me is convinced and blathering incessantly (and then there's something else judging it as blathering...) that almost any decision I make will be a colossally bad decision.

It has collected a very long list of decisions I've made that did not turn out as well as I would have liked. It interrupts every consideration of a big decision with: "Look at the mess you've made of all those other decisions! You are going to make as big a mess, or bigger, this time! And the consequences are going to be even more dire than all the terrible damage of all the past decisions you've made!"

I have come far enough with this to know it is afraid for me. What's troubling is that it recurs and doesn't seem to lessen in intensity no matter how much attention I bring to it. Any advice?

DEAR READER:

Yes, absolutely, this part of you is afraid for you. It's telling you exactly what it is afraid about — that you will make another decision that will mess up your life.

And it hasn't stopped being afraid, even though you have kindly and compassionately let it know that you can hear how afraid it is.

So let's take another angle of approach. Let's make the assumption that this part of you actually has some good reason for how it feels.

It has a list of decisions, and there is something about those decisions that really strikes terror into this part of you. Maybe that would be the next place to bring some interested curiosity.

You might want to sit with that list of decisions in a Focusing way, and let your body give you a felt sense of what they all have in common.

Regrets can be real, and they have a message for you.

I too have a list of decisions that I deeply regret. If I sit with them, I can sense that the decisions were not made from a calm center of Self-in-Presence. With a bit of effort, I am able to bring compassion to the part of me that made those decisions, and made them without making room for me to find my larger, more centered perspective.

I can sense the part of me that was scared, thought I had to decide quickly, thought I didn't have other options. For me, it has to do with a narrow place I can get into where I don't communicate with other people. If I had run any of those decisions past a friend, I would have been much more likely to choose in a way I'd be happy about now.

That brings relief...because I wouldn't mind talking to another person about my current decision. So I realize that what kept that past decision from being a good one, is something I can get in touch with, and use as a source of change.

And the future doesn't have to be like the past.

DO YOU KNOW WHAT TO DO WHEN YOU SIT DOWN TO DO FOCUSING AND YOU GET FLOODED BY EMOTIONS?

"I get flooded by feelings and then, when I try to be Self-in-Presence, I go numb."

Often when I do Focusing, I will get in touch with a felt sense and fairly quickly become flooded by my feelings. I try to move into Self-in-Presence, using what I have learned from you in Inner Relationship Focusing.

I'm not sure if I am getting into Self-in-Presence. I seem to move into a state that is more numb or empty. I try to keep this part company, be curious about "numb," but the process gets stuck there. Do you have any recommendations?

When people are flooded by emotions, Focusing is no longer possible. For Focusing to work, we need to be in a spacious state of Presence, which some people call a clear space.

It is a good idea for you to have a series of moves to support moving into Self-in-Presence. Maybe if one type of move isn't working well, there is another that will work better.

I'm guessing that this state of numbness you describe is a way of escaping from the overwhelming feelings...but not in a way that allows Focusing to happen. To trade overwhelm for numbness allows us to get through the day...but it doesn't allow real change. It's a shutting down, not an opening up.

If a person can get a solid sense of being Self-in-Presence, then there won't be a need to shut down into numbness.

Five simple ways to cultivate Self-in-Presence

1. Grounding. Feel the support of your lower body, sensing your feet, your legs, your buttocks, resting on what you are sitting on.

2. Presence language. Say "I am sensing something in me feels _____."

3. Acknowledging. "I am saying 'Hello' to _____."

4. A gentle hand. "I am letting a gentle hand go there."

5. If necessary, open your eyes, look around the room, feel yourself in the here and now.

Self-in-Presence is the 'I' when you say "I am sensing..." and "I am saying 'Hello.'" When you establish your Self-in-Presence, you are expanding your 'I' — and also your capacity for strength, compassion, and curiosity.

And your capacity for Focusing!

DO YOU EXPERIENCE OVERWHELMING EMOTIONS ALTERNATING WITH DISCONNECTING FROM YOURSELF?

{ *"It seems like all of me doesn't know who she is, and I find it hard to cope."* }

I've been doing your online course for three days now, and today I feel full of emotion and can't seem to get a handle on what's going on. This has been going on for some time, and I'm feeling a bit overwhelmed. I'm very aware that I have been avoiding facing a lot of stuff for a long time, and it's common for me to become impatient with the something in me/disinterested/disconnected....Today when I attempt to approach this, when I bring my hand to it/say "Hello," soon after I disconnect.

Can you suggest anything to help make these feelings more manageable or how to manage the disconnect, because that seems to mean I just switch off, until I feel the emotion rising again and the scenario repeats. I know it's important for me to learn to accept all of me, and this switch off feels so horrible — like the opposite of what I'm trying to do. How could that engender trust for that something in me?

DEAR READER:

In fact, this is the kind of situation for which I created the e-course **Get Bigger Than What's Bugging You** (see p. 85). But as you are discovering, even taking the course may not be enough. Sometimes we need some extra help, so I'm so glad you wrote.

If you are having trouble feeling who YOU are in relation to your emotional states, then the most important sentence is 'I am sensing.' That is the fourth lesson of the course so when you wrote your email you weren't there yet! Even though it is the fourth lesson, for issues like this one where we can start to feel shaky in our sense of our identity, the 'I am sensing' language is the most important of all.

What you experience as disconnecting is a very natural way that our systems handle 'too much' emotion, sort of like a circuit breaker handles too much electrical current. One thing you can do when that happens is say, "I am sensing something in me that needs to disconnect right now." You say it with acceptance, because disconnecting is OK too.

If you sense impatience, same thing. Say, "I am sensing that something in me is impatient." And as you do that, sense in your body, and see if you can feel the difference that that makes when you say it that way.

I know it may not be easy...but being Self-in-Presence can help

The rising up of emotional states and the struggle to disconnect from them is something we can call the 'emotion wars.' These wars cannot be won! The very fact that someone struggles between being taken over by emotion, and on the other hand disconnecting or dissociating, may well be an indication that trauma from the past is affecting the present life.

I hope that saying "I am sensing" and strengthening your sense of Self-in-Presence through grounding — feeling your body resting on support — will help you with this. You might also want to consider having some sessions with a skilled Focusing guide, because we get powerful support for learning self-regulation of emotional states from the accepting presence of another person.

WHAT IF A BODY SENSATION IS UNCOMFORTABLY STRONG, AND IT GETS STRONGER WHEN YOU ACKNOWLEDGE IT?

When a sensation gets stronger instead of releasing...

Last weekend I was Focusing and I felt a pressure on my forehead. The moment I gave a word to it, "pressure," the pressure started to press harder. This surprised me because I usually feel relief the moment I give words to the sense. Something in me wanted it to get softer. I could barely keep my attention with it. I tried things like asking the pressure-part what it needed and setting the pressure at a bigger distance. But the pressure-part kept being really strong. It was a relief to end the session. I had a headache for half an hour after the session.

DEAR READER:

When an uncomfortable sensation gets stronger, it can be a real challenge to our philosophy of 'the radical acceptance of everything!'

Let's remember, though, that our felt experiences come in the way they need to come, in the place and at the intensity that they need to be felt, in order to be met and to carry forward to what is next for them.

If this is true (and I believe it is), then any attempt to change our felt experience from the way it is will simply delay the process of life-forward change.

You were aware, during the process, of another part of you wanting the pressure to get softer. Good for you for being aware of that. What I would recommend next is to invite that part to let you know what it is worried about. You will likely get answers such as, "That this will keep getting worse and worse," and "That I can't do my work if this lasts all day." So then you acknowledge the worries of this part of you. (It usually calms down a bit.)

Now turn back to the uncomfortable sensation. You, as Self-in-Presence, can trust that it is strong like this for some good reason, from its point of view. So turn toward it with compassion and interested curiosity, and say, "I sense you there, and I really sense how strong you are!" Its strength, you see, may well be part of its message.

For example, in a recent Focusing session of this type, the Focuser said, "Oh! I'm sensing that it's afraid if it isn't strong, I am going to ignore it."

What not to do

Saying, "What does it need in order to release?" is something I would not recommend...because the implication is that it should release, and we need to do something to make it do so.

Saying, "I'll try to set it at a bigger distance" is also something I would not recommend. Do you see how that assumes it is not OK as it is?

Really the most transformational thing you can do with any strong felt experience is feel it exactly as it is...really sense into it...and describe it, using fresh metaphors, as if you are encountering it for the very first time ever. This is a method I even use with the pain from a sudden injury. I find that the pain does intensify at first...but as I stay with it, purely sensing and allowing it to be as it is, the experience shifts.

It's when we get identified with an inner struggle with these experiences that they stay the same and don't change.

WHAT DO VULNERABLE TRAUMATIZED PARTS NEED? PROBABLY GENTLENESS AND THE PERMISSION TO GO AS SLOWLY AS THEY NEED TO.

"My dad left our family suddenly and unexpectedly..."

Some of the noticing in my body recently has been of feelings associated with the trauma I experienced as a twelve year old when my Dad left our family suddenly and unexpectedly. I have noticed numbness and vulnerability which I am aware I have very consistently covered by eating sweet things...my comfort at that time. That habit has continued and the feelings I've noticed feel 'old and familiar'...and very fragile as you describe.

Tears are there as I express how slowly and how compassionately I have been acknowledging the feelings over the last two weeks...mostly reassuring them of my company...gently touching my skin...extra gentleness when washing my hands and brushing my hair...making space for the more to come...but not hushing the feelings...or trying to hide them with sugar or carbs. And most importantly, not rushing in and forcing a fixing, which I have been aware of doing in the past. More is coming...I sense it...and this time I am clear that I will be Self-in-Presence to allow the vulnerability to be expressed and the trauma released.

Focusing has led me here and Focusing will continue my healing journey.

DEAR READER:

Wow, what a beautiful recounting of the active gentleness you are bringing to your process! That's a lovely image I have of you washing your hands and brushing your hair with extra gentleness. It really sounds like you are listening to the vulnerable one inside of you and letting her lead the way. You are creating the environment of safety and change by BEING Self-in-Presence, by turning toward what needs attention and allowing it all the time and space it needs. Your story is a beautiful and inspiring one. Thank you so much for giving me permission to share it.

We release trauma by becoming the environment that the traumatized one always needed. It's not hard to do, because compassionate attention is the natural state of Self. It's only parts of us that get impatient and start to say things are not changing quickly enough. And those too we can turn toward and say a gentle "Hello" to. A space of radical acceptance!

CAN FOCUSING HELP WITH PANIC ATTACKS? AT THE LEAST, IT CAN HELP US LISTEN TO THE BODY...

{ *"Ever since the accident, I feel nausea whenever I get in my car."* }

I recently had a car accident. When I drove in my car afterward, I felt pain in the neck and headache and nausea, which have been more or less continuing for about three weeks. I have been getting treatment to alleviate the tension and spasm in the neck and upper body, and there is improvement. But the nausea is getting worse.

After experiencing a profound relaxation during a cranial sacral session, I got back into the car and the nausea and headache became stronger then ever. I stopped the car and Focused. What I heard was: I don't feel safe (in the car and beyond). I couldn't even find another part of me able to say: you are safe.

Today I woke up feeling good, drove five minutes to get a massage and in that short time I got nausea. During the massage I felt fine. As I came home I had a big nausea, and then felt my legs and arms become quite shaky, to the point that standing and walking became uncomfortable. I remember being told that it is a panic attack.

I am not sure how to deal with it...it is uncomfortable and sort of confusing and scary to feel that treatments that help my body relax, bring about this sort of unexpected out-of-control responses. Any suggestion?

DEAR READER:

Yes, I can understand why you would be puzzled. You are getting bodywork treatments to help your body relax, and yet you seem to have even more nausea and discomfort afterward. But what if that makes sense? What if there is something in you that doesn't feel you are safe when driving, so it wants you to be alert... and it gets even more nervous when you are relaxed. Like for this part of you, being relaxed is even more dangerous than not being relaxed!

It occurs to me that rather than having treatments to relax your body (or in addition), you might want to do Focusing with the sensations in your neck and upper body. (I also recommend Somatic Experiencing.) Focusing and SE are a little different from each other but what they both would do is give you a chance to process those activated stress reactions from your accident instead of just relaxing.

To use Focusing, you would spend time compassionately sensing the tension, the nausea, and the one in you that says, "I don't feel safe." You would let it know you really hear it.

You might even feel the rightness of not going in a car until it lets you know that it feels safe enough! This might really change your lifestyle! People would have to come to you. (I hear that grocery stores will make deliveries...)

I'm not talking about giving up on driving. I'm talking about continuing to do Focusing every day, being very accepting, no pushing, just staying with the feel of the physical sensation and being Self-in-Presence for the part of you that doesn't feel safe.

It's important that you are there, that the scared part can feel your steadiness, your calm, your strength.

I wouldn't suggest telling it that it is safe. I would suggest instead telling it that you will be with it every step of the way, as soon as it is ready. And then stay with it.

CAN FOCUSING HELP IF YOU STRUGGLE WITH PAINFUL MEMORIES FROM THE PAST?

A READER WRITES:

Since I've started working on a 2-year-old part that went through some surgery and perceived it as something like abuse/torture/murder/assault, I've been experiencing some mild dissociation. The part blocks me from going further into it because it feels that it's better to keep its memory/knowing out of my sight. It's afraid that once I will know what it knows, although the pain itself will be reprocessed, I will live with that memory forever. It's afraid I will be tormented forever from knowing how what those doctors did destroyed the next twenty years of my life, and that I will never see people the same again. It feels that it's better if I don't know...

I saw an image of a 2-year-old girl locking up the pain in a little locker, and then turning around to me — emotionless, cold, no aliveness left in her...

How do I go from here? The adult part knows it can't live with the intrusive memories, emotional pain, and dissociation anymore...but the child part feels it's better for me to not know what lies deeper at the child's knowing, since it may destroy me and create another feeling about that feeling — anger. As well, I also sense the child itself separated the pain from itself somehow...

DEAR READER:

Everything you are describing is a natural and understandable response to trauma. It is not as well known as it could be, how traumatizing medical operations can be for children. I recommend a book called *Trauma Through a Child's Eyes* by Peter Levine. Levine has worked with many people severely traumatized by medical procedures in childhood. The book also has great advice for parents whose children need to have operations.

When bringing Focusing to a serious issue like this, I feel it is most important to attend to the inner relationship. That means YOU being Self-in-Presence, being the listener, not taking sides with any part. You have described two parts, a child part and an adult part. What you are calling the adult part is still a part. Be sure to say Hello to each one.

Like this: "I am saying 'Hello' to the part of me that doesn't want intrusive memories and dissociation any more, and I am saying 'Hello' to the part of me that feels it is better for me not to know..."

I get the impression, dear Reader, that you feel it is up to you to decide which one of them is right. That will just make you identified with a part again. As Self-in-Presence, we do not decide who is right.

As Self-in-Presence we know something that no part knows. We know that this will change. Parts of us feel scared and urgent for something to happen and tired of the struggle. But change is natural, and the body's own change is ready to happen when there is enough space without pressure.

So be that space. Keep turning toward what is here, allowing it to be as it is. Yes, it has been this way for a long time. But the difference now is that you are here.

WHAT IF YOU ARE IN TOUCH WITH A SCARED PART OF YOU AND YOU HAVE THE URGE TO REASSURE IT, IS THAT A GOOD IDEA?

I'm working through childhood sexual abuse and regularly experience waking from a recurring nightmare. Reading what you wrote to someone else, I realized that it is no wonder that I have been unable to reassure the frightened little girl inside me — because the part of me that has been trying to reassure her is another frightened part — the part that is scared that the nightmare will never end.

I wonder — am I forgetting a key Focusing practice in rushing so quickly to reassure the little girl? Would I be better to try to simply be that space, turn toward the frightened little girl and allow her to be as she is, trusting that in turning toward, she will find her own way through? How does one know when working through something like this when to reassure and when to simply allow?

I want to appreciate you for noticing that the one rushing to reassure the frightened little girl inside is another frightened part. (The key word there is 'rushing'…)

This doesn't mean we shouldn't reassure ourselves, of course. So your question — how does one know when the reassurance is coming from part of us, and when from the whole Self — is a great one.

(Why does it matter? Because if reassurance is coming from another frightened part, it will not actually be reassuring!)

Here is what I would recommend: Be spacious Self-in-Presence, turn toward the frightened little girl, and make a gentle connection with her: "I am here with you." You might let a gentle hand move to where you feel her in your body, to let that contact happen. The touch of the gentle hand is to say "I am here" in a tactile way.

Next invite what kind of contact she would like from you right now. If she asks for reassurance, feel free to give it — because you have been asked. If she asks to be held, give that...but it's equally likely that she may indicate she needs some time, to stand back a bit.

When we are present for what our parts and emotional places need from us, we can be more sure that we haven't gotten identified with 'something' in us that is trying to make the feelings go away by rushing to soothe and fix them.

"Isn't self-soothing a good thing?"

Self-soothing is indeed a good thing! How nice to give ourselves the activities and qualities that we can sense would be needed! That might be anything from an inner hug to a warm bath or a peaceful hour of meditation.

This is where we make the kind of distinction that Focusers love: It's not the activity itself that makes something desirable versus problematic. It's the way we do the action, the place in us from which we do it. So if you discover that the urge to soothe came from a part of you that can't stand how uncomfortable something feels...well, say a gentle 'Hello' to that!

IF YOU STAY IN TOUCH WITH YOUR FEELINGS, DOES THAT INCLUDE THE FEELINGS OF NOT ENJOYING NECESSARY TASKS?

> *"I Focus so much on the feelings of not wanting to do something that I end up not doing it..."*

So in daily life while I'm procrastinating on doing something useful yet challenging, and then I do Focusing with the feelings of not wanting to do it — I actually end up not doing it! Staying true to my feelings makes me quit or procrastinate tasks which I don't enjoy, but which lead to some positive outcomes in future — like making a resume. It looks like I need either something other than just Focusing to get in touch with some motivational energy, or use Focusing correctly — not to 'be' with my feelings that just want relaxation...but maybe to use it somehow to get in touch with some motivation.

Great question! You've discovered something very important...that Focusing is NOT just feeling our feelings. I used to think that was the definition of Focusing, to be aware, to feel how I feel as I am living my life.

But that isn't what Focusing is, and you've put your finger on one of the essential problems with the 'just feeling my feelings' approach....that being in touch with feelings of not enjoying what I am doing might lead to procrastinating on important matters. This is a trap — so let's see how not to get caught in there!

The trouble with "just feeling my feelings" is that then it is very easy to become identified with those feelings. "I am not enjoying this." "I am bored." "I am tired."

"I'll do it tomorrow..." Those are feelings that can easily turn into procrastination, in the absence of Self-in-Presence.

As Self-in-Presence you would say, "I am sensing something in me that is not enjoying this. I am saying 'Hello' to that. Now I am sensing the whole space, my whole self. I can also sense the rightness of going ahead with this now, even though something in me is tired. I am letting it know I really hear how tired it is. OK, that feels better."

Finding motivation with Focusing

Yes, you can use Focusing to get in touch with your motivation!

Take a pause in your task...and first acknowledge compassionately the parts of you that are having a hard time with it. Listen to them for a while...what they tell you might surprise you! For example, a woman in a recent workshop reported: "The part told me it wants to do the writing, it just doesn't want to be pushed." Ah!

Listen from Self-in-Presence until you can feel those parts relaxing because they feel you really heard them.

Now ask your body freshly for a sense of the whole project, inviting the feeling of what you are wanting from doing it. If it's to get a better job, remember what you are wanting to experience from having a new job...and invite your body to give you the feel of that.

This doesn't have to be called a 'part.' Probably the sense of wanting to feel strong, flexible, creative, etc. belongs to your whole Self. So you can say, "I want..." and notice how that feels in your body as if you already have it. This is life carrying forward, and it is likely to carry you forward into the necessary steps of your task.

WHEN YOU ARE HAVING A POSITIVE EXPERIENCE IN FOCUSING, DO YOU HAVE TO SAY "SOMETHING IN ME FEELS..."?

> *"When I or my partner are having a very positive experience, I have the tendency to want to drop the idea of 'something in you' or 'something in me'…"*

When I or my partner are having a very positive experience, such as feeling light coming in, or finding a beautiful place that is very nourishing, I have the tendency to want to drop the idea of 'something in you' or 'something in me' and say "YOU" to the Focuser (if I am Companion) or "I" (if I'm the Focuser and sharing with a Companion).

I get the feeling that these very positive, light giving, nourishing experiences are for my (or the Focuser's) whole being, my (or their) Self-in-Presence.

Do you agree that when these profound positive experiences occur we should not longer talk in terms of Partial Selves?

I do!

I believe that Focusing brings us more and more into an experience of our wholeness. And that can happen…is already happening…at any time. So when we have those positive enjoyable experiences, that is wholeness, not a part.

'Parts' are those narrow aspects of us that are struggling to push or pull us in different directions, driven by some kind of wounding and the attempt to solve the problems the wounding caused (but without the resources to succeed).

What feels difficult, contractive, painful inside is always 'something' that needs compassionate attention.

But what feels flowing, open, alive, at ease, expansive...is not 'something.' It is who we really are.

So when there are enjoyable feelings and life-giving images, you can say, "I feel ____." "I feel joyful and relaxed." And your Companion can say "You feel _____." "You feel filled with light."

DON'T ASSUME THAT YOU KNOW THE MEANING OF AN IMPORTANT LIFE EVENT UNTIL YOU HAVE CHECKED IN WITH YOUR BODY...

"Who knew that was in there?"

A few weeks ago I had the pleasure of witnessing a beautiful transformative Focusing session, and I'd like to share it with you today because it's such a perfect example of what Focusing can do.

My student (we'll call her Doris) started by naming her topic. "I want to Focus today on the subject of my 70th birthday." Anyone listening could tell by the heavy, discouraged tone in her voice that there was no expectation of anything but challenge and heaviness being associated with this landmark occasion.

You would have thought the words "my 70th birthday" referred to a person who had hurt her and would not be forgiven! That was the way the Focusing session started.

"Solidity...strength...wisdom...and flow..."

Doris closed her eyes and started her Focusing session. Rather than staying in her usual thoughts about her situation, she dropped down into body awareness and allowed a fresh whole body sense to come of "my 70th birthday."

When we do this, we are always open to the possibility that our body will surprise us — that the truth is not the same as what we had been thinking. But I've rarely seen a more striking example of this surprise!

Within less than a minute, Doris' voice got calmer and lighter as she described what she was feeling. "In my body I have a sense of solidity...it's feeling very solid in there...in a good way."

She checked if the word "solidity" was a good fit to what she was feeling. "Yes, and now I am also finding a lovely sense of strength..."

Doris paused to enjoy the solidity and strength, but soon was aware of more. "Now I'm feeling something...the word that is coming is 'wisdom.' It's a sense of wisdom. Yes, that's right."

But that wasn't all...Next Doris sensed further and said, "I am feeling a sense of flow in my body now. Flow!" Invited by her Focusing partner, Doris took time to receive and savor these enjoyable feelings, and ended the session with her head shaking in amazement. "Who knew that was there?"

A few weeks later I called Doris to ask about her 70th birthday — what had actually happened. "It was fabulous!" she told me. Everything her body said it would be.

Dear Reader,

I've been writing a Tip per week for the past nine years and am continually inspired and refreshed by the questions people send me. I'd love to hear from you! If you have a question about what you read in this book, or about Focusing or how it can help you, I invite you to write to me at ann@focusingresources.com.

If this is your first encounter with Focusing, I hope you can sense that it could be helpful with many aspects of your life. My company, Focusing Resources, offers a number of classes to help you along with Focusing. If you're just starting out, you might try our **Level One course**. It's a five-week course offered five times per year by phone. If you'd prefer to work with a specific issue, or just one person, we also offer **one-to-one sessions**. In a session, you're guided through the Focusing process in a respectful and supportive way. You can find out more about classes and sessions on our website at focusingresources.com

We also have a library chock-full of free resources on our website, from recordings, to articles, to our **free Get Bigger Than What's Bugging You e-course**. I invite you to visit, have a look around, and see how Focusing can help move your life forward.

May this book bring you support and relief from the challenging areas of your life, and especially fresh hope and more inner and outer resources for moving forward in your life as your full self.

Warmly,